BIGGEST
JOKE
BOOK

Published by Prion Books
An imprint of The Carlton Publishing Group
20 Mortimer Street
London W1T 3JW

ISBN 978-1-85375-738-9

10 9 8 7 6 5 4 3 2

Typesetting by e-type, Liverpool

Printed in the UK by CPI Mackays, Chatham, ME5 8TD

The material in this book was previously published in
Nuts Joke Book and *Nuts Joke Book 2*.

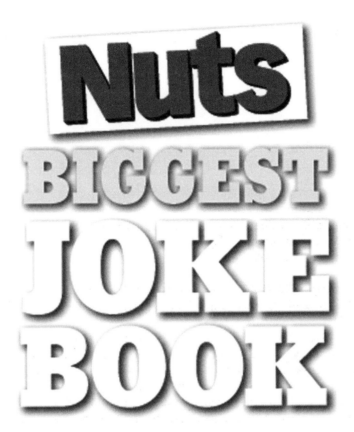

Nuts BIGGEST JOKE BOOK

1,000 JOKES FROM THE UK'S BIGGEST SELLING MEN'S WEEKLY

PRION

From the readers of NUTS

Air traffic self-control

A mother and her young son are on a long-haul flight to America. The son, looking out of the plane's window, turns to his mum and says, "Mum, if big dogs have baby dogs and big cats have baby cats, why don't big planes have baby planes?"

Stumped for an answer, the mother suggests that her son ask the stewardess. The boy promptly gets out of his seat and wanders back to the service area.

"Excuse me," the boy says to the stewardess. "If big dogs have baby dogs and big cats have baby cats, why don't big planes have baby planes?"

"Did your mother tell you to ask me that?"

"Yes," he says.

The stewardess whispers in the boy's ear, "Tell your mother it's because British Airways always pulls out on time."

Sporting chance

What's the difference between a bad golfer and a bad skydiver?

The golfer goes "Thump..." "DAMN!"

Grave concern

A man, his wife and his mother-in-law went on holiday to Jerusalem. While they were there, the mother-in-law passed away. The undertaker told them, "You can have her shipped home for £5,000, or you can bury her here in the Holy Land for £150."

The man thought about it and told him he'd just have her

shipped home. The undertaker asked, "Why would you spend £5,000 to ship your mother-in-law home when it would be wonderful for her to be buried here and you would spend only £150?" The man replied, "Long ago a man died here, was buried here, and three days later he rose from the dead. I just can't take that chance."

Thanks for your support

A Sunderland season ticket-holder calls up the Stadium of Light and asks "What time does the game start?"

The ticket office replies "What time can you get here?"

Tool of the trade

A woman walks into a sex toy store and asks where the vibrators are. "Come this way," the cute woman behind the counter says, gesturing with her finger. "If I could come that way, I wouldn't need the vibrator, would I?" the woman responds.

In a hole

A man loved golf, but his eyesight was so bad he couldn't find his ball once he'd hit it. His wife recommended he take along her uncle, Ted. The golfer said, "But Ted's 80 years old and half-senile!" His wife replied, "Yes, but his eyesight's incredible."

So the man agreed to take Ted along. He teed off and could feel that he'd hit it solidly. He asked Ted, "Do you see it?" Ted nodded his head and said, "Boy, that was a beautiful shot!" The man excitedly asked, "Well, where did it land?!"

Ted said, "Um... I forget."

...Is the right answer!

Brian goes to see his supervisor in the front office.

"Boss," he says, "we're doing some heavy house-cleaning at home tomorrow, and my wife needs me to help with the attic and the garage, moving and hauling stuff."

"We're short-handed, Brian," the boss replies. "I can't give you the day off."

"Thanks, boss," says Brian, "I knew I could count on you!"

How do you tell if a redneck's married? There are tobacco-spit stains on both sides of the truck.

Body language

A couple, who have been married for years, are making love.

He asks, "Dear, am I hurting you?"

"No," she replies. "But why do you ask?"

"You moved," he says.

Better shape up

After passing his driving test, Davey comes home and says, "Dad, can I use the car?"

His dad replies, "OK, son, but first you have to mow the lawn every week for three months and get your hair cut." Three months pass and Davey comes into the house and says, "Dad, the lawn's looked like Lords for the last three months. How about letting me use the car now?" The dad replies, "That's true. But, son, you didn't cut your hair."

So Davey says, "But, Dad, Jesus had long hair!"

"You're right," says Davey's dad. "And he walked everywhere."

Right man for the job

Two MPs are talking late at night in the House of Commons bar.

"How do you choose the right person to back for Prime Minister?" says the younger politician.

"Easy," says the old buffer. "Just adopt the same procedure as you would when choosing a taxi driver."

"What's that?" says the young MP.

"Just decide which one will cost you least and not get you killed."

If it works for you...

A woman spots a little old man sitting happily on a park bench and wanders over for a chat.

"I can't help but notice how happy you look," she says. "What's your secret?"

"Well," replies the man, "I smoke, drink, eat junk food all day and don't exercise..."

"Wow!" replies the woman. "How old are you?"

"Twenty-three."

Tell me again slowly...

Two blokes are lying in bed when one turns to the other and says, "I don't think much of this wife-swapping."

The first cut is the deepest

Feeling uncertain about his love life, a frog calls up a psychic hotline.

"I can see that you're going to meet a beautiful young girl who will want to know everything about you," the psychic tells the frog.

"That's great," the frog says. "Will I meet this babe at a party?"

"No," the psychic says. "In her biology class next term."

Little short of a miracle

A man goes into a shop and sees something he doesn't recognise. He asks the assistant what it is. The assistant replies, "That's a Thermos flask. It keeps hot things hot and cold things cold."

Amazed by this incredible invention, the man buys it immediately.

He walks into work the next day with his new Thermos. His boss sees him and asks, "What's that shiny object?"

"It keeps hot things hot and cold things cold," says the man, proudly.

The boss asks, "What do you have in it?"

"Two cups of tea and some ice-cream," the man replies.

Limited vocabulary

A competition is running on a local radio station.

"Right," says the DJ. "If you can give a word in normal, everyday use that's not in the dictionary then you win £100."

Only one light comes on the phone banks and the DJ punches it quickly.

"Hi, caller. What's your word?" says the DJ.

"GOAN," says the caller.

"How do you spell that?" says the DJ.

"G-O-A-N," the caller replies.

"Well, that's certainly not in the dictionary, but before you get the money can you tell me how you would use it in a sentence?"

"Goan f*** yoursel..." The DJ cuts him off and apologises to his audience for the bad language. Thankfully, another call comes in and the DJ is relieved to be able to move on.

"What's your word, caller?" he enquires.

"SMEE," says the caller.

"And how do you spell that?" says the DJ.

"S-M-E-E," says the caller.

"Well, you're correct SMEE isn't in the dictionary," says the DJ, "but before we give you the money can you tell me how you would use that in a sentence?"

"Smee again," says the caller. "Now goan f*** yourself."

Two chimps in a bath. One says, "Oh, oh, ah, ah, ee, ee!"
The other one says, "Put some cold water in then."

Balance of probabilities

Paul McCartney claims he's not worried about Heather Mills' accusation of wife-beating. He says, "It'll never stand up in court."

That's my girl

Bruce is driving over the Sydney Harbour Bridge one day when he sees his girlfriend, Sheila, about to throw herself off.

Bruce slams on the brakes and yells, "Sheila, what the hell d'ya think you're doing?"

Sheila turns around with a tear in her eye and says, "G'day, Bruce. Ya got me pregnant and so now I'm gonna kill meself."

Bruce gets a lump in his throat when he hears this.

"Strewth, Sheila. Not only are you a great shag, but you're a real sport, too!"

When you gotta go...

A doctor says to his patient: "I have bad news and worse news."

"Oh, dear; what's the bad news?" asks the patient.

The doctor replies: "You only have 24 hours to live."

"That's terrible," says the patient. "How can the news possibly be worse?"

The doctor replies: "I've been trying to contact you since yesterday."

Frequent flier

On the first day of university, the students are told some of the rules: "The female dormitory is out of bounds for all male students, as is the male dormitory to the female students. Anybody caught breaking this rule will be fined £20 the first time. Anybody caught breaking this rule the second time will be fined £60. Being caught a third time will cost you £180. Are there any questions?"

A young male student pipes up: "How much for a season ticket?"

Properly shafted

An agent finds out that his top actress client has been moonlighting as an escort. Having long lusted after her, he asks if he can have sex with her later that night. She agrees, but says, "You'll have to pay like everyone else."

The agent agrees and meets the actress at her house that night. After turning out all the lights, they have sex. The actress falls asleep, but ten minutes later, she is awoken and the scene repeats itself. This goes on for the next few hours.

Eventually, the actress screams out, "This is amazing! I never knew agents were so virile."

A voice from the dark replies, "Lady, I'm not your agent. He's at the door selling tickets."

One-track mind

A man goes to see a psychiatrist, who gives him the inkblot test.

"What does this picture remind you of?" the doctor asks.

"A lesbian nun orgy," the fella replies.

"How about this one?" the shrink asks, holding up another picture.

"A Girls Aloud orgy," the guy says.

After three more pictures, the doctor finally puts down the cards. "You are a sick pervert," he says.

"Me?" the man says indignantly. "You're the one who keeps showing me dirty pictures."

Smart move

God is talking to Adam and Eve one day during the Creation. "Well, you two, I only have a couple more goodies left to hand out before my job is done. Which one of you wants to be able to pee standing up?"

Adam raises his hand and yells "Me, me, pick me!" So God obliges.

God looks at Eve and says: "Well, sorry, Eve... but it looks like you're stuck with the multiple orgasms."

What do Kermit the Frog and Henry the Eighth have in common?
They both have the same middle name.

Sick as a parrot

Raul, Ronaldo and Beckham were all in Real Madrid's canteen, eating their packed lunches. Raul looked at his and said, "Tapas again! If I get tapas one more time, I'm jumping off the top of the Bernabéu."

Ronaldo opened his lunchbox and exclaimed, "Burritos! If I get burritos again, I'll do the same." Beckham opened his lunchbox and said, "Ham and cheese again. If I get a ham and cheese sandwich one more time, I'm jumping too."

The next day, Raul opened his lunchbox, saw some tapas and jumped to his death. Then Ronaldo opened his lunchbox, saw a burrito and jumped too.

Finally, Beckham opened his lunchbox, saw some ham and cheese sandwiches and followed the others in a fatal plunge.

At the funeral, Raul's wife was weeping. She said, "If I'd known how tired he was of tapas, I never would have given it to him again."

Ronaldo's wife also wept and said, "I could have given him tacos or enchiladas! I didn't realise he hated burritos so much."

Everyone turned to Victoria Beckham, dressed in black Versace.

"Hey, don't look at me," said Posh. "David made his own lunch."

Middle stump

Ladies' man Shane Warne is at an Ashes press conference. An Aussie journalist asks, "What would you do if you only had 30 minutes to live, Shane?"

"Ah, mate," he says, "I'd shag the first thing that moved."

The journalist then asks the same question of Freddie Flintoff: "What would you do if you only had 30 minutes to live?"

Freddie eyes Warnie suspiciously and says, "I'd sit very, very still."

And it was good

God, feeling very proud of himself, tells St Peter that he's just created a 24-hour period of alternating light and darkness on earth. "That's clever, God," says St Peter, "what will you do now?"

"Oh, I think I'll call it a day," replies God.

What happens to someone fired from a job at a fairground?
They sue for funfair dismissal.

Good manners

Two old women are sitting in their retirement home.

The first woman says, "When my first child was born, my husband bought me a mansion in Jersey."

The second woman says, "Fantastic."

The other woman brags, "When my second child was born my husband bought me a Rolls-Royce."

"Fantastic," the other woman replies.

"And when my third child was born, my husband bought me the most expensive diamond bracelet they had at Tiffany's."

"Fantastic," says the second old lady.

"So what did your husband buy you when your first child was born?" says the bragging old dear.

"He sent me to charm school," the quiet one replies.

"What the hell for?"

"So instead of saying, 'Who gives a shit?' I could learn to say, 'Fantastic'."

Late developer

On the first day of primary school, the teacher asks everyone to count to 50. Some count as high as 30 or 40; others can't get past 20, but Wayne counts up to 100 without any mistakes. When he tells his dad how well he did, his dad says, "That's because you're an Aussie, son."

The next day, the teacher asks everyone to recite the alphabet. Most can only make it half-way through without trouble, but Wayne rattles off the letters perfectly. When he brags to his dad about how he did, his dad explains, "That's because you're an Aussie, son."

The next day, after games, the boys hit the showers, and Wayne notices that he is better endowed than anyone else. That night he boasts, "Dad, mine's the biggest of anyone in my class. Is it because I'm an Aussie?"

"No, son," explains his dad. "It's because you're 22."

**Why are pirates called pirates?
They just arrrr!**

Man's best friend

Why do men name their penis?

We don't want a total stranger making 90 per cent of our decisions.

Bottoms up

One day, a French spy received a coded message from a British MI6 agent. It read: S370HSSV-0773H.

The spy was stumped, so he sent it to his similarly clueless boss, who forwarded it to Russia. The Russians couldn't solve it either, so they asked the Germans. The Germans, having received this same message during WWII from the Brits, suggested turning it upside down.

The Lord's work

An old nun who lives in a convent next to a construction site notices the bad language of the workers, and decides to spend some time with them to correct their ways.

She decides she'll take her lunch, sit with the workers and talk with them, so she puts her sandwich in a brown bag and walks over to the spot where the men are eating. She walks up to the group and with a big smile says: "Do you men know Jesus Christ?"

They shake their heads and look at each other. One of the workers looks up into the steelwork and yells, "Anybody up there know Jesus Christ?"

One of the steelworkers shouts, "Why?"

The worker yells back, "His wife's here with his lunch."

The capital of America

A girl goes into the doctor's office for a check-up. As she takes off her blouse, the doctor notices a red 'H' on her chest.

"How did you get that mark?" asks the doctor. "Oh, my boyfriend went to Harvard and he's so proud of it he never takes off his Harvard sweatshirt, even when we make love," she replies. A couple of days later, another girl comes in. As she takes off her blouse, the doctor notices a blue 'Y' on her chest. "My boyfriend went to Yale," explains the girl, "and he's so proud of it he never takes off his Yale sweatshirt, even when we make love."

A couple of days later, another girl comes in. She takes off her blouse to reveal a green 'M' on her chest. "Do you have a boyfriend at Michigan?" asks the doctor.

"No, but I have a girlfriend at Wisconsin. Why do you ask?"

Affordable luxury

A couple are walking down the street when the girl stops in front of a jewellery store and says, "Darling, look at that necklace! It's so beautiful."

"No problem," replies her bloke as he throws a brick through the window and grabs the sparkler.

A little later the girl points to a bracelet in the window of another shop.

"Ooh," she says. "I'd love that too!"

"No problem," says her boyfriend and, again, throws a brick through the window.

A little later they pass yet another shop when she sees a diamond ring. "Oh, honey: isn't that lovely?" she says.

"Hang about!" he says. "What do you think I am: made of bricks?"

Mission of mercy

A surgeon was relaxing on his sofa one evening when the phone rang. The doctor calmly answered it and heard the familiar voice of a colleague on the other end of the line. "We need a fourth for poker," said the friend.

"I'll be right over," whispered the surgeon. As he was putting on his coat, his wife asked, "Is it serious?" "Oh, yes, quite serious," said the surgeon, gravely. "Three doctors are there already!"

A boy goes to the Jobcentre and says, "I'd like to work in a bowling alley."
"Ten pin?" says the man behind the desk.
"No, permanent," says the boy.

Hail to the Chief

A man walks into a cowboy bar and orders a beer just as President Bush appears on the television.

After a few sips, he looks up at the television and mumbles, "Now, there's the biggest horse's ass I've ever seen."

A customer at the end of the bar quickly stands up, walks over to him, and decks him.

"Damn it!" the man says, climbing back up to the bar. "This must be Bush country!"

"Nope," the bartender replies. "Horse country!

Cock and bull story

A London lawyer is representing a local train company in a lawsuit filed by a West Country farmer. The farmer's prize bull is missing from the section of field through which the railway passes. The farmer wants to be paid the market price for the bull and just before the case the lawyer immediately corners the farmer and tries to get him to settle out of court. The lawyer does his best selling job, and finally the farmer agrees to take half of what he was asking.

After the farmer signs the release and takes his pay-off, the young lawyer can't resist gloating a little over his success. Outside the High Court he shakes the farmer's hand and tells him, "You know, I hate to tell you this, old fella, but I put one over on you in there. I couldn't have won the case. The driver was asleep when the train went through your farm that morning. I didn't have one witness to put on the stand. I bluffed you!"

The rosy-cheeked farmer replies, "Well, I'll tell you, boy, I was a little worried about winning that case myself, because I'll be blowed if that bull didn't come home this morning."

Warm words

A doctor walks into a bank. Preparing to sign a cheque, he accidentally pulls a rectal thermometer out of his shirt pocket and tries to write with it. Realising his mistake, he looks at the thermometer with annoyance and says, "Well, that's just great. Some asshole's got my pen!"

Swamp thing

A man walks into a pub with his dog on a lead. The landlord
says, "That's a weird-looking dog. He's got stumpy legs, he's pink
and he doesn't have a tail. I bet my rottweiler could beat him in a
scrap." They bet £50 and, out in the backyard, the rottweiler is
soon whimpering for mercy. Another drinker says his pit bull will
win and the bet is increased to £100. Another trip to the
backyard, and when it's all over the pitbull is cowering behind his
owner, who pays up and says, "So what breed is he, anyway?"

The owner says, "Well, until I cut his tail off and painted him
pink, he was the same breed as every other alligator."

Bad medicine

What did the Native American say when the white man tied his
penis in a knot?

"How come?"

Forget I mentioned it

A bloke is in a queue at the supermarket when he notices that
the dishy blonde behind him has raised her hand and is smiling
at him.

He is rather taken aback that such a looker would be waving
to him and, although she's familiar, he can't place where he
knows her from, so he says, "Sorry, do you know me?" She
replies, "I may be mistaken, but I think you might be the father
of one of my children."

His mind shoots back to the one and only time he has been
unfaithful. "Christ!" he says. "Are you that strippergram on my

stag night that I shagged on the snooker table in front of all my mates?" "No," she replies. "I'm your son's English teacher."

> **What did the elephant say to the naked man?**
> **It's cute, but can you pick up peanuts with it?**

Man of the cloth

As the congregation settles into the pews, the preacher walks to the lectern with a red face. "Some one in this congregation," he says gravely, "has spread a rumour that I belong to the Ku Klux Klan."

As a whispering spreads around the hall, the Man of God continues. "This is a horrible lie – one I am embarrassed about and one which a Christian community cannot tolerate. I ask the party who did this to stand up and ask forgiveness from God."

No one moves, so the preacher continues.

"Do you not have the nerve to face me and admit this falsehood? Remember, you will be forgiven and will feel glory in your heart."

Again all was quiet. Then, slowly, a drop-dead gorgeous blonde stands up in the third pew. "Reverend, there has been a terrible misunderstanding. I never said you were a member of the Klan."

"Oh?" says the preacher, "so what did you say?"

The blonde chews her lip and says, "I merely mentioned to a couple of friends that you were a wizard beneath the sheets."

Good for the roses

An American tourist in Dublin decides to duck out of his tour group and explore the city on his own. He wanders around, taking in the sights and occasionally stopping at a quaint pub to soak up the local culture, chat with the lads and have a pint of Guinness. After a while, he finds himself in a very high-class area: big, stately residences, no pubs, no shops, no restaurants and, worst of all, no public toilets.

He really needs to go after all those pints of Guinness and manages to find a narrow side-street – the perfect solution to his problem. As he's unzipping, he's tapped on the shoulder by a policeman, who says, "I say, sir, you simply cannot do that here, you know." "I'm very sorry, officer," replies the American, "but I really, really have to go and I just can't find a public toilet."

"Ah, yes," says the policeman. "Just follow me." He leads him to a back delivery alley, then along a wall to a gate, which he opens. "In there," points the policeman.

"Whizz away, sir. Anywhere you want." The fellow enters and finds himself in the most beautiful garden he has ever seen: manicured grass lawns, statues, fountains, sculptured hedges and huge beds of gorgeous flowers, all in perfect bloom.

Since he has the policeman's blessing, he unburdens himself and is greatly relieved. As he goes back through the gate, he says to the policeman, "That was really decent of you. Is that your famed Irish hospitality?"

"No, sir," replies the cop. "That's what we call the British Embassy."

But I thought you said...

Morris, an 82-year-old man, went to the doctor to get a physical.

A few days later, the doctor saw Morris walking down the street with a gorgeous young woman on his arm.

A couple of days later, the doctor spoke to Morris and said, "You're really doing great, aren't you?"

Morris replied, "Just doing what you said, Doc: 'Get a hot mamma and be cheerful'."

The doctor said, "I said, 'You've got a heart murmur; be careful'."

Blood is thicker...

Redneck Bubba's pregnant sister is in a serious car accident and she falls into a deep coma. After nearly six months she wakes up and sees that she is no longer pregnant. Frantically she asks the doctor about her baby. The doctor replies, "Ma'am, you had twins - a boy and a girl - and your babies are fine. Your brother came in and named them."

The woman thinks to herself, "Oh no! Not Bubba; he's an idiot!" Expecting the worst, she asks the doctor, "Well, what's the girl's name?"

"Denise," the doctor answers with a smile. The new mother thinks, "Wow! That's a beautiful name! I guess I was wrong about my brother. I really like the name Denise."

She then asks the doctor, "What's the boy's name?"

The doctor replies, "Denephew."

On second thoughts...

Three guys are on a trip to Saudi Arabia. One day, they stumble into a harem tent with over 100 beautiful women inside. They start getting friendly with all the women, when suddenly the Sheik storms in.

"I am the master of all these women. No one else can touch them except me. You three men must pay for what you have done today. You will be punished in a way corresponding to your profession."

The Sheik turns to the first man and asks him what he does for a living.

"I'm a policeman," says the first man.

"Then we will shoot your penis off!" says the Sheik.

He then turns to the second man and asks him what he did for a living.

"I'm a fireman," says the second man.

"Then we will burn your penis off!" says the Sheik.

Finally, he asks the last man, "And you: what do you do for a living?"

And the third man answers, "I'm a lollipop salesman!"

Johnny was in class when the teacher farted. Embarrassed, she said, "Johnny, stop that!"

To which Johnny replied, "Which way did it go, Miss?"

Meat is murder

A family was given some venison by a friend. The wife cooked up the deer steaks and served them to the husband and children.

The husband thought it would be fun to have his son guess what it was that they were eating.

"Is it beef?" little Eddie asked.

"No. I'll give you a clue," the dad said. "It's what your mum sometimes calls me."

"Is it useless, pathetic loser?" said Eddie.

As good as new

An Aussie lass is trying to sell her old car but she is having a lot of problems because it has almost 230,000 miles on the clock.

One day, she reveals the problem to her mate.

"There is a possibility to make the car easier to sell, but it's not legal," says her mate.

"That doesn't matter," replies the Aussie lass, "if I can only sell the car."

"OK," says her mate. "Here's the address of a friend of mine. He owns a car repair shop. Tell him I sent you and he'll 'fix it'. Then you shouldn't have a problem any more trying to sell your car."

The following weekend the Aussie lass makes the trip to the mechanic.

About one month after that, her mate asks her, "Did you sell your car?"

"No," replies the Aussie lass. "Why should I? It only has 50,000 miles on the clock."

Rock of ages

What did Keith Richards say after being inducted into the hall of fame? "It's a night I will remember for the rest of the night."

The human condition

Two Arabs boarded a flight out of London. One took a window seat and the other sat next to him in the middle seat. Just before take-off, an American sat down in the aisle seat. After take-off, the American kicked his shoes off and was settling in for the flight when the Arab in the window seat said, "Excuse me. I need to get up and get a Coke." "Don't get up," said the American, "I'm in the aisle seat. I'll get it for you."

As soon as he left, one of the Arabs picked up the American's right shoe and spat in it.

When the American returned with the Coke, the other Arab said, "That looks good; I'd really like one, too." The American went to fetch it and, while he was gone, the other Arab picked up his left shoe and spat in it.

Once the American returned with the drink, they all sat back and enjoyed the flight.

As the plane was landing, the American slipped his feet into his shoes and knew immediately what had happened.

"Why does it have to be this way?" the American asked out loud. "How long must this go on?"

He turned to look at the two Arabs. "All this distrust between our great nations? All this hatred? All this animosity? All this spitting in shoes and pissing in Cokes?"

A classic case

A man walks into a doctor's office. He has a cucumber up his nose, a carrot in his left ear and a banana in his right ear.

"What's the matter with me?" he asks the doctor.

The doctor replies, "You're not eating properly."

What did the sign on the brothel door say?
We're closed. Beat it!

Sole man

A lady goes into a bar and sees a cowboy with his feet propped up on a table. He has the biggest feet she's ever seen. The woman asks the cowboy if what they say about men with big feet is true.

The cowboy replies, "Sure is. Why don't you come back to my place and let me prove it?"

The woman spends the night with him. The next day, she hands the cowboy a hundred dollars. Blushing, he says, "I'm flattered; nobody has ever paid me for my prowess before."

The woman replies, "Well, don't be. Take this money and go buy yourself some boots that fit!"

So now you know

Why wasn't Jesus born in Ireland? Because God couldn't find three wise men or a virgin.

The smart move

A man returns home a day early from a business trip and gets into a taxi at the airport after midnight. On the way back to his house, he asks the cabby if he would be a witness as he suspects his wife is having an affair and he intends to catch her in the act.

For £100, the cabby agrees. They arrive at the house and the husband and cabby tiptoe into the bedroom. The husband switches on the lights, yanks the blanket back and there is his wife in bed with another man.

The husband immediately puts a gun to the naked man's head.

The wife shouts, "Don't do it! This man has been very generous! I lied when I told you I inherited money. He paid for the Porsche I bought for you, your United season ticket, the house at the lake and your golf club membership and green fees."

Shaking his head from side to side the husband slowly lowers the gun and looks over at the cabbie and says, "What would you do?"

The cabby says, "I'd cover him up with that blanket before he catches a cold."

Why do women love men who have been circumcised?

They can't resist something with 20 per cent off!

Number-crunching

Donald Rumsfeld is giving the President his daily briefing on Iraq. He concludes by saying: "Yesterday, seven Brazilian soldiers were killed in an ambush."

"Oh, no! That's terrible!" the President exclaims. His staff sit stunned at this display of emotion, nervously watching as the President sits, head in hands.

Finally, the President looks up and asks, "Um... how many is a brazillion, exactly?"

Eternal optimist

All of Jake's friends always got mad at him because no matter how bad a situation was he would always say, "It could be worse."

Finally his friends decided to make up something that he couldn't say, "It could be worse" about. When they were playing golf one day Steve said to Jake, "Did you hear what happened to Fred?"

"No," said Jake.

"Fred came home Thursday and found his wife in bed with another man, killed them both and then turned the gun on himself."

"It could be worse," said Jake, predictably.

"How could it be any worse than that?" Steve asked.

"Well", Jake said, "If it had happened a day earlier, I'd be dead."

Hop rod

Why was the leper caught speeding?

He couldn't take his foot off the accelerator.

Divine protection

The new vicar's wife had a baby and he appealed to the congregation for a salary increase to cover the new addition to his family.

The congregation agreed that it was only fair, and approved it.

When the next child arrived, the vicar appealed and again the congregation approved the increase.

Several years and five children later, the congregation was getting hacked off with the increasing expenses. This turned into a rather loud meeting one night at the vicarage.

Finally, the vicar stood up and shouted, "Having children is an Act of God!"

An old fisherman in the back stood up and shouted back, "So are rain and snow, but we wear rubbers for them!"

What's the difference between a mechanic and a herd of elephants?
The mechanic charges more.

Death from above

A woman walks into the kitchen to find her husband stalking around with a fly-swatter.

"What are you doing?" she asks.

"Hunting flies," he replies.

"Oh. Killed any?" she enquires.

"Three males and two females," the husband responds.

Intrigued, she asks, "How can you tell?"

"Easy," the husband replies. "Three were on a beer can and the other two were on the phone."

Miscege-nation

On a train from London to Manchester, an American is berating the Englishman sitting across from him in the compartment.

"You English are too stiff. You set yourself apart too much. You think your stiff upper lips make you above the rest of us. Look at me; I have Italian blood, French blood, a little Indian blood and some Swedish blood. What do you say to that?"

"Very sporting of your mother," the Englishman replies.

Holey cow

A farmer is helping a cow give birth when he notices his four-year-old son standing wide-eyed at the fence, witnessing the entire thing.

"Dammit," the man says to himself. "Now I'm going to have to explain about the birds and the bees." Not wanting to jump the gun, the man decides to wait and see if his son asks any questions.

After everything is finished, he walks over to his lad and asks, "Well, son, do you have any questions?"

"Just one," the child says.

"How fast was the calf going when it hit that cow?"

Older is better

Over dinner with the chairman of Ford, Bill Gates starts boasting. "If automotive technology had kept up with computer technology over the past few decades," says Gates, "you could now be driving a V-32 instead of a V-8, and it would have a top speed of 10,000 miles per hour: or you could have an economy car that weighs 30 pounds and gets a thousand miles to a gallon of gas."

"Sure," says the Ford chairman. "But who'd want a car that crashes four times a day?"

Dog and bone

Paris Hilton, filming on location in London, rushes into a local post office. She advances to the counter, flutters her eyelashes and tells the clerk, "I just have to get an urgent message to my mom who's in America."

The clerk informs the heiress that it costs £100 if she wants it sent immediately. She replies, "But I don't have that much cash on me, and I must get a message to her straight away; it's soooo urgent! I'll do anything to get a message to her."

"Anything?" the young clerk asks.

"Yes, anything!" replies the blonde.

He leads her back to the office and closes the door. He tells her to kneel in front of him and unzip his trousers. She does. "Take it out," he says. She does this as well.

She looks up at him, his manhood in her hands, and he says, "Well... what are you waiting for? Go ahead and do it."

Paris brings her lips close to it and shouts, "Hello? Mom?"

Why is Tottenham Hotspur a bit like Kim Wilde?
Glamorous in the Eighties, but not so nice to watch now.

Prize ass

A redneck, named Kenny, buys a donkey from a farmer for $100. The farmer agrees to deliver the donkey the next day.

The next day the farmer drives up and says, "Sorry, son, but I have some bad news; the donkey's dead."

Kenny replies, "Well, then, just give me my money back."

The Farmer says, "I can't do that. I went and spent it already."

Kenny says, "OK, then; just bring me the dead donkey."

The farmer asks, "What are you going to do with him?"

Kenny says, "I'm going to raffle him off."

A month later, the farmer meets up with Kenny and asks, "What happened with that dead donkey?"

Kenny says, "I raffled him off, like I said I was going to. I sold 500 tickets at two dollars a piece and made a profit of $998."

The farmer says, "Didn't anyone complain?"

Kenny says, "Just the guy who won: so I gave him his two dollars back."

A life on the ocean rave

Where do they have parties on a ship?
Where the funnel be.

You had to be there

Three old men were drinking around a pub table. At the table next to them sat a young girl.

The first man said, "I think it's spelt w-o-o-m-b." And the second replied, "No, it must be w-o-o-o-m-b-h." The third said, "No, no, you both have it wrong – it's w-o-o-m." At this, the young lady could stand it no longer. She got up and said, "It's spelt w-o-m-b, you fools." "Listen, love," said one of the old men. "Have you even heard an elephant fart underwater?"

That's telling her

Little Tommy is sitting on a park bench, stuffing a bag of pick-and-mix into his mouth, when an old lady comes over to tell him off. "Son, don't you know that eating all those sweets will rot your teeth and make you sick?"

"My grandfather lived to be 105 years old!" replies Tommy.

"Did he always eat a whole bag of sweets in one go?" the old lady retorts.

"No," answers Tommy, "but he did mind his own business."

Hippocratic oaf

A drunk goes to the doctor complaining of tiredness and headaches. "I feel tired all the time," he slurs. "My head hurts and I'm not sleeping. What is it, Doc?"

Frowning, the doctor examines him before standing back. "I can't find anything wrong," he says. "It must be the drinking."

"Fair enough," replies the lush. "I'll come back when you sober up."

Better luck next time

What does Ashley Giles put in his hands to make sure the next ball almost always takes a wicket?

A bat.

And I think to myself... what a waterfowl world

Three women die together in an accident and go to Heaven. When they get there, Saint Peter says, "We only have one rule here in Heaven; don't step on the ducks."

Sure enough, there are ducks everywhere in Heaven. It is almost impossible not to step on a duck and, although they try their best to avoid them, the first woman accidentally steps on one. Along comes Saint Peter with the ugliest man she ever saw.

Saint Peter chains them together and says, "Your punishment for stepping on a duck is to spend eternity chained to this ugly man."

The next day, the second woman steps on a duck and along comes Saint Peter. With him is another extremely ugly man. He chains them together with the same admonition as he gave the first woman.

The third woman, having observed all this, is very, very careful where she steps. She manages to go months without stepping on any ducks, but one day Saint Peter comes up to her with the most handsome man she's ever seen and, silently, he chains them together. The happy woman says, "Wonder what I did to deserve being chained to you for all of eternity?" The guy says, "I don't know about you, but I stepped on a duck."

Nuts

> **Why do gorillas have red balls?**
> **So they can hide in cherry trees.**

Natural selection

Four men are bragging about how smart their cats are. The first man is an engineer, the second man is an accountant, the third a chemist and the fourth man is a mechanic.

To show off, the engineer calls his cat: "T-square, do your stuff." T-square prances over to the desk, takes out some paper and pen and promptly draws a circle, a square and a triangle. Everyone agrees that he's pretty smart.

However, the accountant thinks his cat can do better. He calls his cat: "Spreadsheet, do your stuff." Spreadsheet goes out to the kitchen and returns with a dozen biscuits. He divides them into four equal piles of three biscuits. Everyone agrees that he's good.

But the chemist says his cat can do better. He calls his cat: "Measure, do your stuff." Measure gets up, walks to the fridge, takes out a pint of milk, gets a 10-ounce glass from the cupboard and pours exactly eight ounces without spilling a drop. Everyone agrees that he's pretty good.

Then the three men turn to the mechanic and ask: "What can your cat do?" The mechanic calls his cat: "Coffee Break, do your stuff." Coffee Break jumps to his feet, eats the biscuits, drinks the milk, craps on the paper, screws the other three cats, claims he injured his back while doing so, files a report for unsafe working conditions and goes home for the rest of the day on sick leave.

The cruel sea

The first mate on a ship decided to celebrate his birthday with some contraband rum. Unfortunately, he was still drunk the next morning. Realising this, the captain wrote in the ship's log: "The first mate was drunk today."

"Captain, please don't let that stay in the log," the mate said. "This could add months or years to my becoming a captain myself."

"Is it true?" asked the captain, already knowing the answer.

"Yes, it's true," the mate said.

"Then, if it's true, it has to go in the log. That's the rule," said the captain, sternly.

A few weeks later, it was the first mate's turn to make the log entries. The first mate wrote: "The ship seems in particularly good shape. The captain was sober today."

Got you there

A married man goes to confession and says to his priest, "I almost had an affair with another woman."

The priest replies, "Almost?"

The man says, "Well, we got undressed and rubbed together; I stopped."

"Rubbing together is the same as putting it in! Say five Hail Marys and put £50 in the poor box."

The man leaves and pauses by the poor box. The watching priest runs over to him saying, "I saw that. You didn't put any money in the poor box!"

The man replies, "Yeah, but I rubbed the £50 on it and, according to you, that's the same as putting it in."

Baggage allowance

Dave says to Phil, "You know, I reckon I'm about ready for a holiday, only this year I'm gonna do it a little different. The last few years, I took your advice as to where to go. Two years ago you said to go to Tenerife; I went to Tenerife, and Marie got pregnant. Then last year you told me to go to the Bahamas; I went to the Bahamas, and Marie got pregnant again."

Phil says, "So what are you gonna do different this year?"

Dave says, "This year, I'm takin' Marie with me..."

Buns for tea

A baker hires a young female assistant who likes to wear very short skirts and a thong. One day a young man enters the store, glances at the assistant and glances at the loaves of bread behind the counter. Noticing the length of her skirt and the location of the raisin bread, he has a brilliant idea.

"I'd like some raisin bread, please," the man says politely. The girl nods and climbs up a ladder to reach the raisin bread, which is located on the very top shelf. The young man, standing almost directly beneath her, gets an excellent view just as he planned. Once she comes down, he says he should get two loaves, as he's having company for dinner.

As the girl retrieves the second loaf of bread, one of the other male customers notices what's going on. Thinking quickly, he requests his own loaf of raisin bread so he can continue to enjoy the view.

With each trip up the ladder, the young lady seems to catch the eye of another male customer. Pretty soon, each male customer is asking for raisin bread, just to see her climb up and down. After many trips she's tired, irritated and thinking that she's really going to have to try the bread herself.

Finally, once again atop the ladder, she stops and fumes, glaring at the men standing below. She notices an elderly man standing among the crowd, staring up at her. Thinking to save herself a trip, she yells at the old man, "Is it raisin for you, too?"

"No," stammers the old man, "but it's quivering a bit!"

Ball skills

A boy walks into a sports shop and tells the staff that he has an amazing talent; he can tell which club emblem any football has printed on it just by feeling it. So the staff blindfold the young lad and hand him a ball.

He feels it and says, "Blackpool. I can smell the sea and feel the sand."

The amazed staff hand him another. He feels it and says, "It's Partick Thistle, I can smell the heather and feel the thistles."

Then they hand him another and he instantly says, "West Ham."

One of the members of staff is amazed, "How did you get that one so quickly?"

"It's going down," the boy replies.

How did Tarzan end up dying?
Picking cherries.

Oopsy!

While attending a convention, three psychiatrists take a walk. "People are always coming to us with their guilt and fears," one says, "but we have no one to go to with our problems. Since we're all professionals, why don't we listen to each other?"

The first psychiatrist confesses, "I'm a compulsive gambler and deeply in debt, so I overcharge patients as often as I can."

The second admits, "I have a drug problem that's out of control, and I frequently pressure my patients into buying illegal drugs for me."

The third psychiatrist says, "I just can't keep a secret."

Damned if you do...

A girl is waiting to enter Heaven when she hears horrible screams of pain and torture coming from inside. She says to St. Peter, "What's going on?" He says, "That's the sound of new angels getting big holes drilled into their backs for their wings, and small holes drilled into their heads for their halos."

She says, "Heaven sounds terrible. I think maybe I'd rather go to Hell."

St. Peter says, "But down there it's hot, smelly and you have to fornicate with anything that moves."

She says, "That's OK; I've already got the holes for that."

Short, sharp shock

Two young guys are picked up by the cops for being drunk and disorderly and appear in court before the judge. The judge tells them, "You seem like nice young men, and I'd like to give you a second chance rather than jail time. I want you to go out this weekend and show others the evils of binge-drinking and get them to give up the booze for ever. I'll see you back in court on Monday."

When the two guys return to court, the judge asks the first one, "So, how did you do over the weekend?"

"Well, Your Honour, I managed to persuade 17 people to give up booze for ever."

"Seventeen people!" says the judge. "That's wonderful. What did you tell them?"

"I used a diagram, Your Honour. I drew a big circle and a small circle and told them that the big circle is your brain without booze and the small circle is your brain after a session."

"That's admirable," says the judge, turning to the second guy. "And you, how did you do?"

"Well, Your Honour, I managed to persuade 156 people to give up alcohol for ever."

"One hundred and fifty six people? That's incredible! How did you manage to do that?"

"Well, I used the same diagram, only I pointed to the small circle first and said, 'This is your asshole before prison...'"

Down, boy

A man takes his cross-eyed dog to the vet. The vet picks him up and examines him for a while and then says, "I'm going to have to put this dog down."

"What? Because he's cross-eyed?"

"No: because he's getting heavy."

> **What's round and snarling?**
> **A vicious circle.**

Present laughter

Four brothers grow up to become wealthy doctors and lawyers. At a meal, they're discussing what gifts they're about to give their elderly mother for her birthday. The first brother pipes up, "I've had a big house built for her."

Another sibling chips in with, "Well, I've had a £100,000 cinema installed in that house for her."

"That's nothing," offers the third brother. "I had my car dealer deliver her a brand-new Ferrari Enzo."

The remaining brother finally speaks up: "You know how Mum loved reading the Bible, but she can't read so well these days? Well, I met this priest who has a parrot that recites the entire book! It took 12 years to teach him – and I've had to pledge to contribute £100,000 to the Church – but I've got him! Mum just has to name the chapter and verse and the parrot will recite it." The brothers are impressed.

Post-birthday, Mum pens some thank-you notes. "David, the house you built is so huge! I live in only one room, but I have to clean the whole place! Not great, but thanks anyway, son." To her second eldest she writes: "Michael, that cinema holds 50 people... but all my friends are dead! I'll never use it. Thank you for the gesture all the same."

"Peter," she writes to her third eldest, "I'm too old to drive, so I never use the Enzo. The thought was kind. Thanks."

Finally, the youngest boy receives his letter: "Dearest Richard! You were the only son to have the good sense to put a little thought into your gift. The chicken was absolutely delicious!"

Snot a problem

A man and a woman are sitting next to one another on a flight to New York. The woman sneezes, takes out a tissue, wipes her nose and then shudders for about ten seconds. A few minutes later, the woman sneezes again. Once more, she takes a tissue, wipes her nose and then shudders. A few more minutes pass before the woman sneezes and shudders again. Curious, the man says, "I can't help noticing that you keep sneezing and shuddering. Are you OK?"

"I'm so sorry if I disturbed you," says the woman. "I suffer from a condition that means whenever I sneeze, I have an orgasm."

"My God!" says the man. "Are you taking anything for it?"

"Yes," says the woman. "Pepper."

Time and punishment

The cops are ordered to clean up the High Street for a big parade, and are patrolling the pavements when a drunk staggers towards them. "Excuse me, offisher," he says to one constable, "could you pleash tell me the time?"

The constable frowns at him. "One o'clock," he says, before whacking him once over the head with his truncheon.

"Christ!" says the drunk, reeling. "I'm glad I didn't ask you an hour ago!"

Curry On Doctor

With a screech of brakes, an ambulance pulls up at the local casualty ward and a hippie is wheeled out on a hospital trolley. The doctor questions the man's hippie friends about his situation.

"So what was he doing then?" asks the physician. "Acid? Cannabis?"

"Sort of," replies one of the hippies, nervously thumbing his kaftan, "but we ran out of gear, so I skinned up a home-made spliff."

"And what was in that?" asks the doctor.

"Um… I kind of raided my girlfriend's spice rack," says the hippie. "There was a bit of cumin, some turmeric and a little paprika."

"Well, that explains it," the doctor replies, looking at them gravely. "He's in a korma."

Top of the plops

Two flies land on a steaming heap of manure.

The first lifts his leg and farts.

The other fly says, "Jesus, Jim; I'm trying to eat."

Animal magnetism

An Aussie walks into his bedroom with a sheep under his arm and says: "Darling, this is the pig I have sex with when you have a headache."

His girlfriend, lying in bed, says: "I think you'll find that's a sheep."

The man replies: "I think you'll find I wasn't talking to you."

Pier pressure

Every morning a man took the ferry to work. One morning, he woke up and found he had no electricity. He had no idea what time it was, but assumed he was late since he had a tendency to sleep late anyway.

So he scoffed down his breakfast, rushed to the port where he saw the ferry ten feet from the dock, and took a running leap. He barely made it, skidding across the deck of the boat, and hurt himself quite badly. "You know," said the captain, "in another minute we would have docked."

Why don't men fake orgasms?
Because no man would pull those faces on purpose.

It was worth a try

A mild-mannered man is tired of his wife always bossing him around, so he decides to be more assertive. When he gets home from work, he says to his wife, "From now on, I'm the man of this house. When I come home from work, I want my dinner on the table. Now go upstairs and lay me some clothes on the bed, because I'm going out with the boys tonight. Then draw my bath.

And, when I get out of the tub, guess who's going to dress me?"

"The undertaker?" she replies.

> Two rats in a sewer talking to each other. One says to the other, "I'm sick of eating sh*t."
>
> The other rat says, "It's OK, I've spoken to the lads – we're on the p*ss tomorrow."

Once bitten...

A guy walks into a bar with his pet monkey. He orders a drink and the monkey runs around before grabbing some olives off the bar and eating them. Next he eats the sliced lime before he jumps up on the pool table, grabs the cue ball and swallows it whole.

The barman yells, "Did you see what your monkey just did?"

"No, what?" replies the man.

"He just ate the cue ball off my pool table - whole!"

"Yeah, that doesn't surprise me," replies the patron. "He eats everything in sight, the little twerp. I'll pay for the cue ball and stuff." He finishes his drink, pays his bill, and leaves.

Two weeks later he returns with his monkey. He orders a drink and the monkey starts running around the bar again.

While the man is drinking, the monkey finds a maraschino cherry on the bar. He sticks it up his butt, pulls it out, and eats it. The bartender is disgusted. "Did you see what your monkey did now?"

"What?" asks the riled drinker.

"He stuck a maraschino cherry up his bottom, then pulled it out and ate it!"

"Yeah, that doesn't surprise me either," replies the man. "He still eats everything in sight, but ever since he ate that damn cue ball he measures everything first!"

Struck down in his prime

A man tells his doctor he's unable to do all the things round the house that he used to. After an examination, he says, "Tell me in plain English what's wrong with me, Doc."

"Well, in layman's terms, you're lazy," says the doctor.

"OK. Now give me a medical term, so I can tell my wife."

Cometh the hour, cometh the man

A fire starts inside a chemical plant and the alarm goes out to fire stations miles around. After crews have been fighting the fire for more than an hour, the chemical company president approaches the fire chief and says, "All our secret formulae are in the vault. They must be saved. I'll give £100,000 to the firemen who bring them out safely." Suddenly, another engine comes roaring down the road and drives straight into the middle of the inferno. The other men watch, unbelieving, as the firemen hop off their engine and heroically extinguish the fire, saving the secret formulae. The company president walks over to reward the volunteers and asks them, "What do you fellas plan to do with the money?"

The driver looks him right in the eye and answers, "Well, the first thing we're going to do is fix the brakes."

Top marks for thinking

Little Johnny is in a class where every Friday the teacher asks a question and if you get it right you don't have to go to school on Monday.

The first Friday the question is, "How many gallons of water are there in the whole world?"

No one knows so they all have to go to school on Monday.

Next Friday, the question is, "How many grains of sand are there in the whole world?"

Again, the class is clueless so they have to go to school on Monday.

Now Little Johnny is getting angry because he doesn't want to go to school on Monday, so he paints two ping-pong balls black.

The next Friday right before the teacher asks her weekly question Johnny rolls the two balls up to her.

Angrily, the teacher asks, "OK, who's the comedian with two black balls?"

Little Johnny replies: "Chris Rock. See you Tuesday!"

Q: What's black and white and red all over?
A: A cow that's just been murdered

It's funny because it's true

How do you know if you've caught bird flu? You're suddenly unable to park and all you can talk about is shoes.

Who's the king of the hankies?
The handkerchief.

Ewe get yer own!

An Australian is on holiday in New Zealand and is walking through a farm when he comes across a New Zealander having sex with a sheep.

The Australian says to the New Zealander, "In Australia we shear them."

The New Zealander looks horrified. "I'm not shearing this with nobody!"

Eve of destruction

In the beginning, God created the earth and rested.

Then God created Man and rested.

Then God created Woman.

Since then, neither God nor Man has rested.

Figure of fun

On his first night in prison, a convict is glumly eating his dinner when another inmate jumps to his feet, shouts, "Thirty-seven!" and all the other inmates laugh hysterically. Another shouts back, "Four hundred and twenty!" and gets the same reaction.

"What's going on?" says the new inmate to his cellmate.

"It's like this," says the convict. "We only have one joke book in this prison and everyone knows all the jokes off by heart, so instead of telling the whole joke, we just stand up and shout out a page number."

A few days later, the new convict decides that it's time to join in, so he stands up and shouts, "Fourteen!"

Total silence ensues. Turning to his cellmate, he asks, "What went wrong?"

The convict replies, "It's the way you tell 'em."

The Great and Powerful

Former Presidents Bill Clinton and George Bush Snr are travelling through Kansas with George Bush Jnr.

A tornado comes along and whirls them up into the air and tosses them thousands of miles away. They all fall into a daze. When they come to and stumble out of the limousine, they realise they're in the fabled Land of Oz.

They decide to go see the famous Wizard of Oz, known for granting people their wishes.

Bush Jnr says, "I'm going to ask the Wizard for a brain."

Bush Snr responds, "I'm going to ask the Wizard for a heart."

Clinton thinks for a moment, and says "Where's Dorothy?"

Why did Frosty the Snowman get excited?
He heard the snowblower coming.

It's a tuft job, but someone's got to do it

A bloke goes into the Jobcentre in London and spots a job vacancy which reads, "Wanted: single man, willing to travel, must have own scissors. £500 a week guaranteed, plus company car and all expenses."

It sounds a bit too good to be true, so the bloke fronts up at the counter and quotes the job's reference number.

"Oh, that one," says the clerk. "It's a modelling agency here in London. They're looking for a pubic hair snipper. They supply girls who model underwear and before they go on the catwalk they report to you to snip off any wisps of pubic hair that are showing. It pays well, but there are drawbacks; it involves a lot of travel to exotic places and you have to get used to living in first-class hotels." "Well, I'd still like to apply," says the bloke. The clerk says, "OK, here's an application form and a rail ticket to Manchester."

"What do I wanna go to Manchester for?" "Well," says the clerk, "that's where the end of the queue is at the moment."

From here to maternity

What did the Aussie lass say to the doctor when she got pregnant?
  Are you sure it's mine?

Local knowledge

A Scotsman, an Englishman and an Aussie are having a drink in America.

"Y'know" says the Scotsman, "I still prefer the pubs back home. In Glasgow there's a little bar called McTavish's. Now the landlord there goes out of his way for the locals so much that when you buy four drinks, he'll buy the fifth one for you."

"Well", says the Englishman, "at my local, the Red Lion, the barman there will buy you your third drink after you buy the first two."

"Ahhhhh, that's nothing", says the Aussie. "Back home in Sydney there's Bruce's Bar. Now, the moment you set foot in the place they'll buy you a drink, then another, all the drinks you like. Then, when you've had enough drinks, they'll take you upstairs and see that you get laid, and it's all on the house."

The Englishman and Scotsman immediately scorn the Aussie's claims. But the Aussie swears every word is true.

"Well," says the Englishman "has this actually happened to you?"

"Not me personally, no," says the Aussie. "But it did happen to my sister."

Epic journey

After a DIY store sponsored Ellen Macarthur's solo sea voyage, a man went into the store to congratulate them. "Well done for getting a yacht to leave the UK on November 28, 2004, sail 27,354 miles around the world and arrive back 72 days later," said the man. "Absolutely amazing."

"Well, thank you," replied the startled employee. "Now, is there any chance you could let me know when the kitchen I ordered 96 days ago will be delivered from your warehouse 13 miles away?"

Slow food

Three tourists were driving through Wales. As they were approaching Llanfairpwllgwyngyllgogerychwyrndrob-wllllantysiliogogogoch, they started arguing about the pronunciation of the town's name. They argued back and forth until they stopped for lunch.

As they stood at the counter one asked the blonde employee, "Before we order, could you please settle an argument for us? Would you please pronounce where we are... very slowly?"

The girl leaned over the counter and said, "Burrrrrrgerrrrrr Kiiiiiing."

Without a prayer

One night before bed, Arsène Wenger is trying to think of ways to get Arsenal's season back on track. As a last resort, he prays to God. God hears his prayers and decides to take pity. Later that night, Wenger suddenly awakes to see the Lord in front of him.

"Come forth, my son!" says the Lord.

To which Wenger replies, "Fourth? We'll be lucky if we finish bloody fifth."

Circle of friends

What does Britney say after sex?

"Are you boys all in the same band?"

Eugh!

A cowboy and an Indian are riding their horses together when they both stop and jump down. The Indian lies flat on the floor and puts his ear to the ground.

"Buffalo come!" cries the Indian.

"How do you know that?" asks the cowboy, impressed.

"Easy: ear stuck to ground," the Indian replies.

Body language

BB King's wife wants to surprise him for his birthday, so she goes to a tattoo parlour and has a big 'B' tattooed on each of her buttocks.

When BB gets home later that night, he opens the door to find his wife naked and bent over showing off her new tattoos. BB can't believe his eyes and screams, "Who the hell's Bob?"

How many kids with Attention Deficit Hyperactivity Disorder does it take to change a light bulb?
Wanna ride bikes?

Bungle in the jungle

Alan Curbishley goes on a scouting mission to the South American rainforest. When he arrives he spots a huge local tribesman standing in a clearing. Suddenly a huge seedpod drops from a tree and the man volleys it with incredible power and precision through a tiny hole in the foliage.

"Bloody hell!" says Curbs. "Can you do that again?"

So the tribesman does exactly the same thing, only this time he juggles the pod from foot to foot before blasting it through the hole in the foliage.

Needless to say, Curbishley signs up the tribesman from the rainforest and proudly shows him off at the next West Ham training session.

"Before we go any further," says Curbs, "Ball" (pointing at the ball); "Goal" (pointing at the goal). "That's Ball and Goal."

"But, boss," protests the tribesman, "I can speak perfect English."

"I know that," replies the desperate manager, "I was talking to the rest of the team."

Scrotal recall

A man is lying in bed in the hospital with an oxygen mask over his mouth. A young nurse appears to sponge his hands and feet.

"Excuse me, nurse," he mumbles from behind the mask, "Are my testicles black?"

Embarrassed, the young nurse replies, "I don't know; I'm only here to give you a bed-bath."

He struggles again to ask, "Nurse, are my testicles black?" Finally, she pulls back the covers, raises his gown, holds his penis in one hand and his testicles in her other hand and takes a close look, and says, "There's nothing wrong with them."

Finally, the man pulls off his oxygen mask and replies,

"That was very nice, but are... my... test... results... back?"

Stupid bankers

Roman Abramovich walks into a bank in London and asks to see the manager. "I'm going to Moscow on business for two weeks and need to borrow £5,000," says Roman.

The manager replies, "I'm afraid we'll still need some kind of security for the loan."

"No problem," says the Blues' boss and hands over the keys to his brand new Bentley.

The bank agrees to accept the car as collateral for the loan and the manager and the tellers all enjoy a good laugh at the Russian's expense for using a £200,000 car as collateral against a £5,000 loan. An employee of the bank then proceeds to drive the Bentley into the bank's underground garage and parks it there. Two weeks later, Roman returns, repays the £5,000 and interest, which comes to £15.41.

The manager says, "We are very happy to have had your business, Mr Abramovich, and this transaction has worked out very nicely, but we are a little puzzled. Why would you bother to borrow £5,000? You're one of the richest men in the world."

Roman replies, "Where else in London can I park my car for two weeks for only £15.41 and expect it to be there when I return?"

Full of clap

Bono's fronting the home leg of U2's latest world tour in Dublin when he asks the audience for some quiet. Then he starts to slowly clap his hands and, as he does so, says into the microphone, "Every time I clap my hands, a child in Africa dies."

A voice from near the front pierces the silence, "Well, stop f**king clapping, then!"

Dream come true

Three blokes, an Englishman, a Frenchman and a Welshman, are out walking along the beach. They come across a lantern and a genie pops out of it. "I will give you each one wish!" cries the genie.

The Welshman says, "I'm a farmer, my dad was a farmer, and my son will also farm. I want the land to be for ever fertile in Wales."

With a blink of the genie's eye, 'FOOM' – the land in Wales is for ever made fertile for farming.

The Frenchman is amazed, "I want a wall around France, so that no one can invade our precious country," he says.

Again, with a blink of the Genie's eye, 'FOOM' – there is a huge wall around France.

The Englishman asks, "I'm very curious. Please tell me more about this wall."

The Genie explains, "Well, it's about 150 feet high, 50 feet thick and nothing can get in or out."

The Englishman says, "Fill it up with water."

Encountering turbulence

A guy sitting at a bar at Heathrow notices an attractive woman sitting next to him. He thinks to himself: "Wow, she's so gorgeous she must be a flight attendant. But which airline does she work for?"

Hoping to pick her up, he leans towards her and utters the Delta Airways slogan: "Love to fly and it shows?"

She gives him a blank, confused stare.

A moment later, the Singapore Airlines slogan pops into his head. He leans towards her again, "Something special in the air?"

She gives him the same confused look.

Next he tries the Thai Airways slogan: "Smooth as silk."

This time the woman turned to him and said, "What the fuck do you want?"

The man smiles, slumps back in his chair, and says "Ahhhhh: Air New Zealand!"

What do politicians do when they die? Lie, still!

Braking the habit

One day, a mechanic was working under a car when some brake fluid accidentally dripped into his mouth. "Wow," said the mechanic to himself. "That stuff tastes good." The following day, he told his mate about his discovery.

"It tastes great," said the mechanic. "I think I'll try a little more today."

The next day, the mechanic told his mate he'd drunk a pint of the stuff. His friend was worried but didn't say anything until the next day, when the mechanic revealed he'd drunk two pints.

"Don't you know that brake fluid is toxic? It's really bad for you," said his mate.

"I know what I'm doing," snapped the mechanic. "I can stop any time I want to."

Vow of silence

A mafia godfather finds out that his bookkeeper has swindled him out of ten million dollars. This bookkeeper is deaf, so the godfather brings along his attorney, who knows sign language.

The godfather asks the bookkeeper, "Where's the ten million you embezzled from me?"

The attorney, using sign language, asks the bookkeeper where the money is hidden.

The bookkeeper signs, "I don't know what you're talking about."

The attorney tells the godfather: "He says he doesn't know what you're talking about."

At this point, the godfather pulls out a 9mm pistol, puts it to the bookkeeper's temple, cocks it and says, "Ask him again!"

"He'll kill you if you don't talk," signs the attorney.

The bookkeeper signs back: "OK. You win! The money is buried in my cousin Enzo's back yard."

The godfather asks the attorney, "Well, what'd he say?"

The attorney replies, "He says you don't have the balls..."

When push comes to shove

After hearing a couple's complaints that their sex life isn't what it used to be, the sex counsellor suggests they vary their position.

"For example," he says, "you might try the wheelbarrow. Lift her legs from behind and off you go."

The eager husband is all for trying this new idea as soon as they get home.

"Well, OK," the hesitant wife agrees, "but on two conditions. First, if it hurts you have to stop right away, and second you have to promise we won't go past my parents' house."

**What do you call cheese that's not yours?
Nachocheese.**

The majesty of the law

After listening to an elderly prostitute plead her case, Judge Poe calls a brief recess and retires to his chambers. En route, he bumps into a colleague, Judge Graham.

"Excuse me, Judge Graham," Poe asks. "What would you give a 63-year-old prostitute?" "Let me think," Judge Graham replies. "Ten quid, tops."

Legend in his own lifetime

An artist asks a gallery-owner if there's been any interest in his paintings recently.

"I have good news and bad news," the gallery owner tells him. "The good news is a gentleman enquired about your work and wondered if it would appreciate in value after your death. When I told him it would, he bought all 15 of your paintings."

"That's great," the artist says. "What's the bad news?"

"He was your doctor."

Toad in the hole

Walking down the high street, a woman spies a shop doorway she's never seen before. Pinned to the front is a sign: "Lady pleasing frog – inside."

Checking to make sure no one's watching, she darts in – only to find an almost bare room. "Er, can you help me?" she asks the man behind the counter. He looks up and grins widely, "Oui, mademoiselle!"

Gotcha!

Two Aussies, Wayne and Shayne, go camping. They pack a cooler with sandwiches and beer and set off. After two days of hiking, they arrive at a great spot but soon realise that they've forgotten to pack a bottle opener.

Wayne turns to Shayne and says, "You gotta go back and get the opener or else we have no beer."

"No way, mate," says Shayne. "By the time I get back, you'll have eaten all the food."

"I promise I won't," says Wayne. "Just hurry!"

Five full days pass and there's still no sign of Shayne. Exasperated and starving, Wayne gives in to hunger and digs into the sandwiches. Suddenly, Shayne pops out from behind a rock and yells, "I knew it! I'm not f**king going!"

Doctor, Doctor

One night, a man and a woman are at a bar downing a few beers. They strike up a conversation and quickly discover that they're both doctors. After about an hour, the man says to the woman, "Hey, how about we sleep together tonight? No strings attached. It'll just be one night of fun."

The woman agrees. So they go back to her place. She goes into the bathroom and starts scrubbing up like she's about to go into the operating room.

She scrubs for a good 10-20 minutes. Finally, she goes into the bedroom and they have sex for an hour or so. Afterwards, the man says to the woman, "You're a surgeon, aren't you?"

"Yeah, how did you know?" she replies.

"I could tell by the way you scrubbed up before we started," he says.

"Oh, that makes sense," says the woman.

"You're an anesthesiologist, aren't you?"

"Yeah," says the man, a bit taken aback. "How did you know?"

The woman answers, "I didn't feel a thing!"

Increasing frustration

The Hunchback of Notre Dame returns home from a hard day's ringing the cathedral bells, and finds his beautiful wife standing in the kitchen holding a wok.

"Fantastic, Esmeralda," says the Hunchback, "I really fancy some Chinese food."

"Oh, no, not tonight, Quasi," she says, "I'm ironing your shirts."

> **What do the Inland Revenue, an ostrich and a pelican all have in common?**
> **They can all stick their bills up their arses.**

Beastly behaviour

A gorilla and a rhino are best mates until one day, as the rhino bends over to drink at the watering hole the gorilla takes advantage of the situation and jumps him from behind. The rhino is furious and chases the gorilla all over the savannah. Half an hour later, still being chased by the rhino, the gorilla spots a tourist sitting in a chair, reading a newspaper. Quick as a flash, he knocks the tourist unconscious, strips him, hides him in the bush, puts on his clothes and sits down in his chair. Moments later, the rhino comes charging past and asks:

"Have you seen a gorilla around here anywhere?"

Holding the paper up to hide his face, the gorilla replies: "What, the one that rogered the rhino by the watering hole?"

"Oh, shit," says the rhino, "don't tell me it's in the papers already."

Plucked if I know

What's the difference between kinky and perverted?

Kinky is using the feather; perverted is using the chicken.

Every home should have one

A man walks into a pub with a small doll in his hand and says to the barmaid, "What's this?"

He then pokes the doll in the stomach and a man in the corner of the pub screams. Without saying a word, the man then leaves.

The next day, the man walks back in the pub at the same time, and says to the same barmaid, "What's this?"

He pokes the doll in the stomach as before and, once again, a man in the corner screams. As the man is about to leave again, the barmaid shouts, "I don't know. What is it?"

"Déja voodoo," replies the man.

Calls from mobiles may cost more

Several men are in the changing room of a golf club when a mobile phone on a bench rings and a man answers. He switches to hands-free and everyone else in the room stops to listen.

"Hello," says the guy.

A female voice answers, "Honey, it's me. Are you at the club?"

"Yes," replies the man.

"I'm at the shops now and found this beautiful leather coat. It's only £1,000. Is it OK if I buy it?"

"Sure, go ahead if you like it that much," says the guy, nonchalantly.

The woman goes on. "I also stopped by the Mercedes garage and saw the new models. I saw one I really liked."

"How much?" enquires the man.

"£60,000," says the spendthrift.

"OK, but for that price I want it with all the options," says the fella.

"Great!" says the woman. "Oh, and one more thing. The house we wanted last year is back on the market. They're asking £950,000."

"Well, then go ahead and give them an offer, but just offer £900,000," replies the man.

"OK. I'll see you later! I love you!" the woman signs off.

"Bye, I love you, too," says the man and hangs up.

The other men in the changing room look at him in astonishment.

Then the man asks: "Anyone know whose phone this is?"

We'll cashew one day...

An elderly couple had a parlour in which they kept a couple of food bins. One of those bins contained apples, and the other bin contained nuts. They were having quite a bit of trouble with mice, so one evening before going to bed they set a couple of mouse traps, one by the bin of apples and one by the bin of nuts. During the night they heard a trap snap. The old gentleman got up to see which mouse trap had caught a mouse.

On returning to bed his wife asked, "Well, did we catch him by the apples?"

The old gentleman replied, "Nope. Try again."

Natural disaster

How are tornadoes and marriage alike?

They both begin with a lot of blowing and sucking, and in the end you lose your house.

Why, you little...

A guy is driving down the road at 100mph singing, "Twentyone today, twenty-one today!" Soon, a cop pulls him over and says, "Because it's your birthday, I'll let you off." Despite the cop's warning, the guy screeches off and is soon doing a ton down the road again. The cop, in hot pursuit, then sees the man mow down a traffic warden. Suddenly, the man starts singing, "Twenty-two today, twenty-two today!"

What's the definition of a happy transvestite?
A guy who likes to eat, drink and be Mary.

Accident victim

A woman and a man driver are involved in a horrific collision, but amazingly both escape unhurt - though their cars are written off.

As they crawl out of the wreckage, the man sees the woman is blonde and strikingly beautiful. Then the woman turns to the man and gushes: "That's incredible, our cars are demolished but we're fine. It's a sign from God that we're meant to be together!"

Sensing a promise, the man stammers, "Yes, I agree!"

The woman continues, "And look; though my car was destroyed, this bottle of wine survived! It must be another sign. Let's drink to our love!"

"OK!" says the man, going with the moment. She offers him the bottle, he downs half of it and hands it back.

"Your turn," says the man.

"No, thanks," she replies, "I think I'll just wait for the police."

Tales from the crypt

Late one night, a young chap was walking home from a club. Most of the streetlights in the area were broken. Suddenly, he heard a strange noise. Startled, he turned and saw a coffin following him. He started to jog, but he heard the coffin speed up after him. Eventually, he made it to his front door, but he knew the coffin was only seconds behind. He dived inside, slamming the front door behind him. Suddenly, there was a crash as the coffin smashed its way through the front door. In horror, the young lad fled upstairs to the bathroom and locked the door. With an almighty smash, the bathroom door flew off its hinges and the coffin stood in its place. Desperate, the young man reached into his bathroom cabinet. He grabbed a bar of Imperial Leather soap and threw it at the coffin, but still it came. He grabbed a can of Lynx deodorant and threw it, but still it came. Finally, he threw some cough mixture. The coffin stopped.

For I have sinned

A drunken man staggers into a Catholic church, sits down in the confessional and says nothing. The bewildered priest coughs to attract his attention, but still the man says nothing.

The priest then knocks on the wall three times in a final attempt to get the man to confess. Finally, the drunk replies, "No use knockin', mate; there's no paper in this one either."

See you later, applicator

Two young boys go into a pharmacy, pick up a box of Tampax and walk to the counter.

"How old are you, son?" inquires the pharmacist.

"Eight."

"Do you know how these are used?"

"Not exactly," says the boy, "but they aren't for me. They're for my brother; he's four. We saw on TV that if you use these you'll be able to swim and ride a bike, and he can't do either."

Crack of dawn

Why is getting up at three in the morning like a pig's tail?

It's twirly.

Skin game

A man is working at the zoo when his boss says, "The gorilla is sick today and it's the busiest day of the year – you'll have to put on this gorilla suit so as not to disappoint the public."

"No chance," says the man.

However, his boss warns him that if he doesn't put on the suit and pretend to be the gorilla he'll be sacked.

Grudgingly, the man gets dressed and jumps into the gorilla's cage. After a while he starts to enjoy it and begins showing off. Without warning, his tyre swing snaps and he lands in the lion's den. The male lion pounces on him and starts mauling the man, who begins screaming for his life.

Suddenly he hears the lion say, "Shut up or we'll both get the sack!"

Beggars can't be choosers

Two friends were playing golf when one pulled out a cigar. He didn't have a lighter, so he asked his friend if he had one. "Yep," he replied and pulled out a 12-inch Bic lighter from his golf bag.

"Wow!" said his friend. "Where did you get that monster?" "I got it from the genie in my golf bag."

"You have a genie? Could I see him?"

The other bloke opens his golf bag and out pops a genie.

The friend asks the genie, "Since I'm a friend of your master, will you grant me one wish?"

"Yes, I will," the genie replies. The friend asks the genie for a million bucks and the genie hops back into the golf bag and leaves him standing there, waiting for his million bucks.

Suddenly, the sky darkens and the sound of a million ducks flying overhead is heard.

The friend tells his golfing partner, "I asked for a million bucks, not a million ducks!"

He answers, "I forgot to say; he's a bit deaf. Do you really think I asked him for a 12-inch Bic?"

What do you call a bear without a paw? A bastard.

Child's play

What is the similarity between PlayStations and breasts?

Both are made for children, but used by adults.

Beyond a choke

A man walks through a big shopping centre with his teenage son.

The boy tosses a 50p up in the air and catches it between his teeth to impress his dad, but he fails to clamp down with his teeth and ends up choking on the money. As the boy coughs and wheezes the father panics and shouts, "Help! Is there a doctor in the house? My son's choking!"

Not too far from the action, a man sitting in a cafe reading a paper hears the father's cries and patiently puts down his coffee and folds his paper. He then walks over to the boy, grabs him by the balls and squeezes the hell out of them.

The startled lad immediately coughs up the 50p and the man catches it in his hand and walks away.

The amazed father runs over and says, "Thank you, sir; you saved my son's life. Are you a doctor?"

"No," the man replies, "I work for HM Revenue and Customs."

Hairy moment

A man walks into a restaurant and orders a cheeseburger.

Later, the waitress brings his meal to him. He takes a bite out of it, and notices there's a small hair in the hamburger. He begins yelling frantically at the waitress, "Waitress, there's a hair in my hamburger! I demand to see what's going on!"

So the waitress takes him to the kitchen and, to his horror, he sees the cook take the meat patty and flatten it under his armpit. He says, "That's disgusting!"

The waitress replies, "You think that's disgusting? You should see him make doughnuts."

Hear, hear

Sadly, Dave was born without ears, and though he proved to be successful in business, his problem annoyed him greatly.

One day he needed to hire a new manager for his company, so he set up three interviews. The first man was great. He knew everything he needed to know and was very interesting. But at the end of the interview, Dave asked him, "Do you notice anything different about me?"

"Why, yes; I couldn't help but notice that you have no ears," came the reply. Dave didn't appreciate his honesty and threw him out of the office.

The second interview was with a woman, and she was even better.

But he asked her the same question: "Do you notice anything different about me?"

"Well," she said, stammering, "you have no ears."

Dave again got upset and chucked her out in a rage.

The third and final interviewee, a young student, was the best of the bunch.

Dave was anxious, but went ahead and asked the young man the same question: "Do you notice anything different about me?"

Much to Dave's surprise, the young man answered, "Yes; you wear contact lenses, don't you?"

Dave was shocked. He'd finally found the perfect person for the job.

"How in the world did you know that?" he asked delighted.

The young man fell off his chair, laughing hysterically, and replied, "Well, it's pretty hard to wear glasses with no bloody ears!"

> **Hear about the flasher who was thinking of retiring?**
> **He's sticking it out for a while longer.**

A night to remember

As Claude the hypnotist took to the stage, he announced, "Unlike most stage hypnotists, I intend to hypnotise each and every member of the audience."

Claude then withdrew a beautiful antique pocket watch from his coat. "I want you each to keep your eye on this antique watch. It's a very special watch. It has been in my family for six generations."

He began to swing the watch gently back and forth while quietly chanting, "Watch the watch. Watch the watch. Watch the watch. Watch the watch. Watch the watch..."

Hundreds of pairs of eyes followed the swaying watch – until, unexpectedly, it slipped from Claude's fingers and fell to the floor, breaking into a hundred pieces.

"Sh*t!" exclaimed the hypnotist, loudly. It took three weeks to clean the seats.

Reversal of fortune

A man goes into a bar and sees a friend at a table, drinking by himself.

"You look terrible," says the man. "What's the problem?"

"My mother died in August," says the friend, "and left me £25,000."

"Gee, that's tough," replies the man.

"Then in September," the friend continues, staring deep into his glass, "my father died, leaving me £90,000."

"Wow! Two parents gone in two months. No wonder you're depressed."

"And last month my aunt died, and left me £15,000."

"Three close family members lost in three months. How sad," says the man in a comforting tone.

"Then this month," his friend goes on, "absolutely nothing!"

Heated debate

A man is in a butcher's in Glasgow. The butcher is out the back, by a radiator. The man is looking at the counter and shouts, "Is that your Ayrshire bacon?"

The butcher shouts back, "No, I'm just warming my hands."

You're in

A little old lady decides she wants to join a bikers' club, so she goes to a meeting of the local Hells Angels. A big, bearded, leather-clad biker opens the door and asks what she wants. "I want to join your club," she tells him. Deciding to humour her, he asks if she has a bike. "Over there, in the car park," she replies, pointing to a shiny new Harley.

"And do you drink?" he asks.

"Like a fish," she says. "I can drink any bloke under the table." The biker is now suitably impressed.

"OK," he asks. "But have you ever been picked up by the fuzz?"

"No!" comes the reply. "But I have been swung around by the nipples a few times."

Fair question

The instructor at a pregnancy and labour class is teaching the young couples how to breathe properly during delivery. The teacher announces, "Ladies, exercise is good for you. Walking is especially beneficial. And, gentlemen, it wouldn't hurt you to take the time to go walking with your partner." The room falls quiet. Finally, a man in the middle of the group raises his hand. "Is it all right if she carries a golf bag while we walk?"

All mod cons

A salesman checks into a futuristic hotel. Needing a haircut before his meeting, he calls reception to see if there's a barber on the premises.

"I'm afraid not, sir," the receptionist tells him, "but down the hall from your room is a vending machine that should serve your purposes."

Sceptical but intrigued, the salesman locates the machine, inserts £10 and sticks his head into the opening, at which point the machine starts to buzz and spin. Fifteen seconds later, he pulls out his head and looks in the mirror to see the best haircut of his life.

"That's amazing," he says before noticing another machine with a sign reading, "For 50p this machine will provide a service men need when away from their wives..." Very excited, he skips the rest of the description, and puts the coin in the slot.

"Oh, man. Do I ever need this!" he gasps, looking both ways and unzipping his fly. When the machine starts buzzing, he lets out a shriek of agony and almost passes out. Fifteen seconds later, it shuts off. With trembling hands, the man withdraws his member, which now has a button neatly sewn on the end.

Have you heard about the new super-sensitive condom?
It hangs around after the man leaves and gives the woman a hug.

Teed off

A golfer is about to tee off when he's approached by a man holding out a card that reads, "I am a deaf mute. May I please play through?"

The guy gives the card back, angrily shaking his head. Assuming the guy can lip-read, he adds, "I can't believe you would try to use your handicap for a cheap advantage like that! Of course you can't play through!"

The deaf man walks away and the guy whacks the ball on to the green and then walks off to finish the hole.

Just as the golfer is about to putt out, he's hit in the head with a golf ball that knocks him out cold.

When he comes to a few minutes later, he looks around and sees the deaf mute sternly looking at him, one hand on his driver, the other hand holding up four fingers.

Shatterday mourning

What do you get after five days of non-stop sex? A weak end.

Nuts

All passion spent

One misty Scottish morning a man is driving down from Wick
to Inverness. Suddenly, a huge red-haired highlander steps into
the middle of the road. At the roadside there also stands a
beautiful woman. The driver's attention is dragged from the
girl when the highlander opens the car door and drags him
from the seat.

"Right, you," he shouts. "I want you to masturbate."

"But..." stammers the driver.

"Now, or I'll bloody kill you!"

So the driver starts to masturbate. Thinking of the girl at the
roadside, this only takes a few seconds.

"Right," says the highlander, "do it again!"

"But..." says the driver.

"Now!" shouts the highlander.

So the driver does it again.

This goes on for two hours until, finally, the driver collapses
in an exhausted heap.

"Again!" says the highlander.

"I can't," whimpers the man. "You'll just have to kill me."

The highlander looks down at the man slumped on the
roadside.

"All right," he says, "now you can give my daughter a lift to
Inverness."

Tooled up

After years of stuttering, Jim finally goes to the doctor to see if
he can be cured. The doctor thoroughly examines him, and
asks him to drop his pants – whereupon Jim's massive member

78

thuds on to the table. "Hmm," says the physician. "I see the problem – because of gravity your penis's weight is putting too much strain on the vocal chords in your neck."

"B-b-b-ut wh-wh-at c-c-c-an b-b-be d-done?" asks Jim.

The doctor smiles. "Don't worry. Modern surgery can work miracles. We can replace your penis with one of normal size and the stuttering will instantly disappear."

Convinced, Jim agrees to the op – and as the doctor promised, his stuttering completely stops afterwards. About three months later, however, he returns to the doctor's surgery. "Doc, I'm still grateful for what you did," he says, "but my wife really misses the size of my old member. So I've decided I'll live with stuttering for the rest of my life, and get my old dick back."

The doctor shakes his head, sadly. "Hey," he says, "a d-d-de-deal's a d-d-deal."

Taking precautions

After several unsuccessful years of searching for Mr Right, a woman decides to take out a personal ad. She ends up corresponding with a man who has lived his entire life in the Australian Outback; and, after a long-distance courtship, they decide to get married.

On their wedding night, she goes into the bathroom to prepare for the festivities. When she returns to the bedroom, she finds her new husband standing in the middle of the room, naked and all the furniture from the room piled in one corner.

"What's going on?" she asks.

"I've never been with a woman," he says. "But if it's anything like a kangaroo, I'm going to need all the room I can get!"

Above us the waves

How do you sink a US Navy submarine?
  Knock on the hatch.

Not so sweet

A Jelly Baby goes to the doctor. "Doctor, doctor; I think I've got an STD."

The doctor is surprised, "You can't have an STD, you're a Jelly Baby!"

"But, doctor, I've been sleeping with Allsorts."

What do you call an insect that flies around a lampshade at 180mph?
Stirling Moth.

Aw, shucks

What did the redneck get on his IQ test?
  Drool.

For I have sinned

What kind of fun does a priest have?
  Nun.

Decisions, decisions

A woman goes into a dentist's office and, after her examination, the dentist says to her, "I'm sorry to tell you this, but I'm going to have to drill that tooth."

Horrified, the woman replies, "Oh, no! I'd rather have a baby." The dentist replies, "Make up your mind; I have to adjust the chair."

Moving in a mysterious way

What's the difference between Ronaldo and God?

God doesn't think he's Ronaldo.

The outer limits

What did the camp Dalek say?

Effeminate! Effeminate!

First the bad news...

In the middle of poker night John loses a £500 hand, clutches his chest, and drops dead on the floor. His mate Pete is designated as the guy who has to go and give his wife the bad news.

"Be gentle with her, Pete," one of the other players says. "They were childhood sweethearts."

So Pete walks over to John's house, knocks on the door, and tries his best to be helpful. "Your husband just lost £500 playing cards."

"Tell that idiot to drop dead," shouts the wife.

"I'll tell him," Pete says.

A nip in the air

What's another name for push-up bras?
  False advertising.

Finger-licking bad

What's the difference between a conference footballer and a KFC bucket?
  The KFC can feed a family of four.

How do you get 500 cows in a barn?
Put up a sign saying 'Bingo'.

Shedding your load

What does an Aussie use for protection during sex?
  A bus shelter.

Land of my Godfathers

Did you hear about the Welsh Mafia boss?
  He'll make you an offer you can't understand.

In-car entertainment

A man buys a new car, but returns the next day, complaining that he can't figure out how the radio works. The salesman explains that the radio is voice-activated.

"Watch this!" he says... "Beatles!"

Sure enough, Eleanor Rigby starts blaring from the speakers.

The man drives away happy, and for the next few days, every time he says a band's name he gets their greatest hits.

One day, a dangerous driver runs a red light and nearly creams his high-tech car, but he swerves in time to avoid them.

"Assholes!" he yells. All of a sudden the German national anthem, sung by Coldplay, comes on the radio...

Monkey business

A man walks into a bar and sees a monkey in a cage.

He asks the bartender, "What does the monkey do?"

The barman says, "I'll show you." He opens the cage door, hits the monkey on the head with a cricket bat and the monkey gives him oral scx.

The man is amazed and the bartender says, "You want to have a go?"

"Definitely," says the man, "but you don't need to hit me so hard."

Paradise island

A retired corporate executive decides to take a holiday. He books himself on a Caribbean cruise and proceeds to have the time of his life – that is, until the ship sinks. He finds himself on an island with no other people, no supplies, nothing. After about four months, he is lying on the beach when the most gorgeous woman he has ever seen rows up to the shore.

In disbelief, he asks, "Where did you come from? How did you get here?"

She replies, "I rowed from the other side of the island. I landed here when my cruise ship sank."

"Amazing," he notes. "You were really lucky to have a row boat wash up with you."

"Oh, this thing?" explains the woman. "I made the boat out of raw material I found on the island. The oars were whittled from gum tree branches. I wove the bottom from palm branches, and the sides and stern came from a eucalyptus tree."

"But, where did you get the tools?" asks the amazed castaway.

"Oh, that was no problem," replies the woman. "On the south side of the island, a very unusual stratum of alluvial rock is exposed. I found if I fired it to a certain temperature in my kiln, it melted like iron. I used that for tools and used the tools to make the hardware." The guy is stunned.

"Let's row over to my place," she says. After a few minutes of rowing, she docks the boat at a small wharf. As the man looks to shore, he nearly falls off the boat. Before him is a stone walk leading to an exquisite bungalow painted in blue and white.

Trying to hide his continued amazement, the man accepts a drink, and they sit down on her sofa to talk.

"I'm going to slip into something more comfortable," says the woman. She soon returns wearing nothing but vines, strategically positioned. She beckons for him to sit down next to her.

"Tell me," she begins suggestively, "We've been out here for many months. You've been lonely. There's something I'm sure you've been longing for…" She stares into his eyes.

He can't believe what he's hearing. "You mean," he swallows excitedly and tears start to well in his eyes, "you've built a kebab shop?"

Cut to the chase

A man walks into an antiques shop. After a while, he chooses a brass rat and brings it to the counter. "That will be £10 for the brass rat and £1,000 for the story behind it," says the owner. "Thanks, but I'll pay the £10 and pass on the story," replies the man.

So the man buys the brass rat and leaves the shop. As he walks down the street, he notices all sorts of rats following him. The further he walks, the more rats follow. He walks down to the pier and still more rats come out and follow him. So, he decides to walk out into the water and all the rats drown. Afterwards, he goes back to the shop.

"Ah-ha, you're back!" says the owner. "You've come back for the story, right?"

"Nope," says the man. "You got any brass lawyers?"

Nuts

Holy matrimony

On their way to get married, a young couple are involved in a fatal car accident. The couple find themselves sitting outside the Pearly Gates waiting for St. Peter to process them into Heaven. While waiting, they begin to wonder; could they possibly get married in Heaven? When St. Peter shows up, they ask him.

St. Peter says, "I don't know. This is the first time anyone has asked. Let me go and find out."

He goes off to get to the bottom of it. The couple sit down to wait for an answer... for a couple of months. St. Peter finally returns looking somewhat bedraggled.

"Yes," he informs the couple, "you can get married in Heaven."

"Great!" says the couple, "But we were just wondering, what if things don't work out? Could we also get a divorce in Heaven?"

St. Peter, red-faced with anger, slams his clipboard on to the ground.

"What's wrong?" ask the frightened couple.

"Come on!" St. Peter shouts. "It took me three months to find a priest up here! Do you have any idea how long it'll take me to find a lawyer?"

What's black and white and eats like a horse?
A zebra.

Look on the bright side

A group of OAPs were sitting around talking about their various ailments.

"My arms are so weak, I can hardly hold this cup of coffee," said one.

"Yes, I know," replied another.

"My cataracts are so bad I can't even see my coffee."

"I can't turn my head because of the arthritis in my neck," said a third, to which several nodded weakly in agreement.

"My blood pressure pills make me dizzy," another went on.

"I guess that's the price we pay for getting old," winced an old man.

Then there was a short moment of silence. "Well, it's not that bad," said one woman cheerfully.

"Thank God we can all still drive!"

Second opinion

An old fella with a dodgy heart goes to see his doctor about some chest pains he's been experiencing.

When he gets home his wife asks him if he's been prescribed medication. "No, nothing like that," says the old man. "I'm going to make some lunch."

Wanting to give him some space, the wife lets her husband go. Ten minutes later she hears screams of pain coming from the kitchen and rushes in to find the old guy cooking a fry-up in a biscuit tin and burning his fingers whenever he touches it.

"What on earth are you doing?" she screams.

"Just following doctor's orders," says the old man. "He said the best thing I can do for my heart is to throw away the frying pan."

Law of nature

A female TV reporter arranges for an interview with a farmer, seeking the main cause of Mad Cow disease. "Good evening, sir. I am here to collect information on possible causes of Mad Cow disease. Can you offer any reason for this disease?" she asks.

The farmer stares at the reporter, "Do you know that a bull mounts a cow only once a year?" he asks.

The embarrassed reporter replies: "Well, sir, that's a new piece of information, but what's the relation between this phenomenon and Mad Cow disease?"

"And, madam, do you know that we milk a cow twice a day?" he asks, ignoring her.

"Sir, this is really valuable information, but what about getting to the point?" she retorts.

"I am getting to the point, madam. Just imagine; if I was playing with your breasts twice a day and only having sex with you once a year, wouldn't you get mad?"

Subterranean dipstick blues

What do you get if you put Coldplay in your basement?
A whine cellar.

That deserves some sort of prize

A married man was having an affair with his secretary. One day, their passions overcame them and they went to her house, where they made love. Afterwards, they fell asleep, only waking up at 8pm. As the man threw on his clothes, he told the woman to take his shoes outside and rub them through the grass and dirt. Mystified, she went ahead and did it. He then slipped into his shoes and drove home.

"Where have you been?" demanded his wife when he entered the house.

"Darling, I can't lie to you," he said. "I've been having an affair with my secretary and we've been having sex all afternoon. I fell asleep and didn't wake up until eight o'clock." The wife glanced down at his shoes and said, "You lying bastard! You've been playing golf."

What do you call 12 naked men sitting on each others' shoulders?
A scrotum pole.

Loyal support

What will you get if Man United are relegated this season?
About 70,000 more Chelsea fans.

The spirit is willing, but...

One afternoon, an elderly couple are relaxing in front of the TV. Suddenly, the woman is overcome with lust and says to her husband, "Let's go upstairs and make love." "Steady on," he replies. "I can't do both."

The shellfish gene

One day, in the shark-infested waters of the Caribbean, two prawns called Justin and Christian are discussing the pressures of being a preyed-upon prawn.

"I hate being a prawn," says Justin "I wish I were a shark."

Suddenly a mysterious cod appears. "Your wish is granted" he says.

Instantly Justin becomes a shark. Horrified, Christian swims away, afraid his former friend might eat him. As time passes, Christian continues to avoid Justin, leaving the shrimp-turned-predator lonely and frustrated. So when he bumps into the cod again, he begs the mysterious fish to change him back. Lo and behold, Justin is turned back into a prawn. With tears of joy in his tiny little eyes, he swims back to the reef to seek out Christian.

As he approaches, he shouts out: "It's me, Justin, your old friend. I've changed... I've found Cod. I'm a prawn again, Christian."

My mum said never marry a tennis player.

Love means nothing to them.

Slip-up

A boy comes home from school looking sheepish. "Dad," he moans, "we had a class spelling contest today, and I failed on the very first word."

"Ah, that's OK, son," says his father, looking over his glasses at him. "What was the word?"

The son looks miserable. "Posse," he replies.

His father bursts out laughing. "Well, no wonder you couldn't spell it," he roars. "You can't even pronounce it."

Stripped for action

A soldier at the Pentagon gets out of the shower, and realises that his clothes are missing. He searches around for them, but accidentally locks himself out of his locker room, and finds himself completely naked in the halls of the world's most powerful military organization HQ. But, luckily, no one is around to see him.

So he runs as fast as he can to the elevator. When it arrives, it's empty. He breathes a sigh of relief and gets in. When the doors open on his floor, there is no one waiting outside. "This must be my lucky day," he says to himself. He is now only a few yards from his office.

Suddenly, he hears footsteps coming from around the corner. He hears the General's voice. There is no way he'll make it to his door in time, so he ducks into the closest office available, and finds himself in the laboratory for Research & Development. The Head Scientist looks up from one of her experiments with puzzled interest.

The soldier thinks quickly, stands up straight and salutes.

"I am here to report the partial success of the Personal Invisibility Device," he says.

"I see," the Head Scientist says. "The Shrink Ray seems to be working perfectly, too."

> **Why did the horse win the Nobel Prize?**
> **Because he was out standing in his field.**

Honest mistake

A man was sprawled out across three entire seats in his local cinema. When the usher came by and noticed this, he whispered to the man, "Sorry, sir, but you're only allowed one seat." The man groaned but didn't budge, and the usher became impatient. "Sir," the usher repeated, "if you don't get up from there, I'm going to have to call the manager."

Again, the man just groaned, infuriating the usher, who then turned and marched briskly back up the aisle in search of his manager. In a few moments, both the usher and the manager returned and stood over the man. Together the two of them tried to move him, but with no success. Finally, they decided to call the police. Soon, a policeman arrived and surveyed the situation briefly.

"Alright, mate. What's your name?"

"Sam," the man moaned.

"Where you from, Sam?" the cop asked.

"The balcony."

Monstrous regiment

Why is getting a new girlfriend like joining the army?

You're forced to have a new haircut, a new set of clothes, and you only get information on a need-to-know basis.

Oval Orifice

What will history remember Bill Clinton as?

The President after Bush.

Whoopee!

Jack and Bob are driving when they get caught in a blizzard. They pull into a nearby farmhouse and ask the attractive lady of the house if they can spend the night. "I'm recently widowed," she explains, "and I'm afraid the neighbours will talk if I let you stay here."

"Not to worry," Jack says. "We'll be happy to sleep in the barn."

Nine months later, Jack gets a letter from the widow's attorney. After reading it, he quickly drives around to Bob's house.

"Bob, remember that good-looking widow at the farm we stayed at?"

"Yes, I remember her," says Bob.

"Did you happen to get up in the middle of the night, go up to the house and have sex with her?" asks Jack.

"Yes, I have to admit that I did," replies Bob. "Did you happen to use my name instead of telling her your name?" asks Jack.

Embarrassed, Bob says, "Yeah, I'm afraid I did."

"Well, thanks a lot, pal," says Jack. "She just died and left me her farm!"

With a hey-nonny-no

Why can't you circumcise a Morris dancer?

Because they have to be complete dicks.

The truth hurts

Tired of a listless sex life, a husband asks his wife during lovemaking "How come you never tell me when you have an orgasm?"

To which she replies, "You're never here!"

Bliss eternal

Two brothers, Brian and Phil, make a deal that whichever one dies first will contact the living one from the afterlife. Brian dies a few years later. Phil doesn't hear from him for about a year and ruefully figures that there is no afterlife.

Then one day he gets a call. It's Brian. "So there is an afterlife! What's it like?" asks Phil.

"Well," begins Brian. "I sleep really late. I get up, have a big breakfast, then I have sex – lots of sex. Then I go back to sleep, but I get up for lunch, have a big lunch and have some more sex – lots more sex. Then I take a nap: then a huge dinner and loads more sex. Then I go to sleep and wake up the next day."

"Oh, my God," says Phil. "Heaven sounds amazing!"

"I'm not in heaven," says Brian. "I'm a lion in Windsor Safari Park."

The old enemy

Before an England vs Scotland friendly, Wayne Rooney goes into the England changing room, only to find all his team-mates looking a bit glum. "What's the matter, lads?" he asks. "We're having trouble getting motivated for this game, Wayne," replies Becks. "We know we're playing for national pride but it's only Scotland. We can't really get all that excited."

Rooney looks at them and says, "Well, I reckon I can beat them single-handed. You lads have the afternoon off and watch from the pub."

So Rooney goes out to play Scotland all by himself and the rest of the squad nip off to the pub for a few pints. After a few jars they wonder how the game is going, so they get the landlord to put it on the TV. A big cheer goes up as the screen reads, "England 1 – Scotland 0 (Rooney, 10 minutes)". A few more pints of lager later, and Ashley Cole shouts out, "It must be full-time now, let's see how he got on."

They look up at the TV and see "England 1 (Rooney, 10 minutes) – Scotland 1 (Ferguson, 89 minutes)". The England team can't believe it – Rooney has managed a draw against the entire Scotland team. They all rush back to the stadium to congratulate him but find him in the dressing-room, sobbing, with his head in his hands. He refuses to look at them.

"I've let you down, lads," says Rooney.

"Don't be daft!" says Becks. "You got a draw against Scotland all by yourself, and they only scored in the 89th minute!"

"No, no. I have let you down," insists Rooney. "I got sent off in the 12th minute."

What should you do if you're attacked by a gang of clowns?
Go for the juggler.

Sheer brass neck

Every day, Tony Blair jogs past a prostitute who stands on the same street corner near the Houses of Parliament. "Two hundred and fifty quid for you, Tony!" she shouts from the kerb.

Embarrassed, the Prime Minister feels he has to shout something just to shut her up, so he yells: "No! A fiver!"

This ritual soon becomes a daily occurrence.

One day, Cherie Blair decides that she wants to accompany her husband on his daily jog. As the couple nears the working woman's street corner, Tony realises she will bark her £250 offer and Mrs B will wonder what he's really been doing on all his past outings.

As the pair jogs into the turn that takes them past the corner, the premier becomes even more apprehensive than usual.

Sure enough, there is the prostitute. Tony tries to avoid her eyes as she watches the pair jog past but amazingly, she doesn't say anything. Tony can't believe his luck. Then suddenly from her corner, the hooker yells after them, "See what you get for a fiver?"

Cold reception

A woman walks into an ice cream parlour and orders a scoop of chocolate ice cream.

The owner shakes his head apologetically and says, "I'm sorry, but we're all out of chocolate."

The lady looks confused and gazes down through the glass at all the ice cream tubs and then looks back up at the man and asks for a cornet of chocolate ice cream. The man replies a little annoyed, "Er, I'm sorry, but we're all out of chocolate."

The lady then seems to get the point and walks down to the

end of the parlour. She then looks back up and says, "Excuse me? Can I get a litre of chocolate ice cream?"

At this point the owner explodes, "Miss, do me a favour please? Can you spell the 'straw' in strawberry?"

"Sure," says the woman. "S-T-R-A-W."

"Now can you spell the 'Van' in Vanilla?" says the owner.

"Yes. V-A-N," the lady says confidently.

"Now can you spell the F*ck in chocolate?" the owner says smartly.

The lady looks up at the ceiling in thought then replies, "There is no F*ck in chocolate."

"Exactly!" screams the owner.

Narrow escape

A little guy goes into an elevator, looks up and sees a huge bloke next to him. The man sees the little fella staring at him, looks down and says, "Seven feet tall, 350 pounds, 20-inch penis, three-pound left testicle, three-pound right testicle, Turner Brown." The small guy immediately faints and falls to the floor.

The tall man kneels down and brings him to, slapping his face and shaking him. "What's wrong with you?" he asks. In a very weak voice, the little guy says, "Excuse me, but what exactly did you say to me?"

The tall man answers, "I saw the curious look on your face and figured I'd just give you the answers to the questions everyone always asks me. I'm seven feet tall, 350 pounds, 20-inch penis, three-pound left testicle, three-pound right testicle, and my name is Turner Brown." "Thank God for that," the small guy says. "I thought you said, 'Turn around'."

If you think it'll help...

A husband and wife visit a counsellor after 15 years of marriage.

The counsellor asks them what the problem is and the wife starts ranting, listing every problem they've had during their marriage. She goes on and on and on; suddenly the counsellor gets up, walks around the desk and kisses her passionately. The woman shuts up immediately and sits in a daze. The counsellor turns to the husband and says, "This is what your wife needs at least three times a week. Can you do this?"

The husband thinks for a moment and replies, "Well, I can drop her off here on Mondays and Wednesdays, but on Fridays, I'm out drinking."

How is sex like air?
It's not a big deal unless you're not getting any.

Mucky ducky

A woman is taking a stroll through the woods when a little white duck, covered in filth, crosses her path.

"Let me clean you," the woman says, taking a tissue from her purse.

The woman walks on a little further and encounters another duck, also with muck all over it. Again, she produces a tissue and cleans the bird. Afterwards, she hears a voice from the bushes.

"Excuse me, madam," it says. "Do you have any more tissues?"

"No!" the woman replies, offended.

"All right," the voice says. "I'll just have to use another duck, then."

Using your loaf

"We specialise in hygiene" said the sign at the bread shop and the customer was delighted when he saw the baker use tongs to pick up his rolls and put them in a bag.

"Untouched by human hands!" said the baker. "Very good," said the customer as he immediately started to eat one of the rolls. "But tell me – what's that piece of string hanging out of your flies?"

"Hygiene," said the baker. "When I have a pee, I pull it out with the string."

"How do you put it back?" asked the customer. "With the tongs, of course," replied the baker.

Mutual satisfaction

A man drives his date up to Lovers' Lane and parks up.

"I have to be honest with you," the woman says as the man makes his move. "I'm a prostitute."

The man thinks about this for a bit and decides he's OK with it. He agrees to pay her £25 in advance and they get down to business.

After they finish, the man says, "Now, I should be honest, too. I'm a taxi driver and it's going to cost you £25 to get back into town."

And that's magic

Three Essex girls are flying back from an exotic holiday when their plane crashes into the sea. The three survive and are washed up on a deserted island. They've been stranded for days when they find a magic lamp. They rub it and eventually a genie pops out.

"Since I can only grant three wishes," he says, "you may each have one."

Number one says, "I've been stuck here for days. I miss my family, my husband, and my life. I just want to go home."

She disappears in a flash and is returned to her family.

Number two then says, "I've been stuck here for days as well. I miss my local boozer and Friday night kebabs. I want to go home too."

She vanishes as well, and finds herself back down the pub.

Suddenly, number three starts crying uncontrollably.

The genie asks, "My dear, what's the matter?"

She whimpers, "I'm lonely. I wish my mates were still here."

Where do you get virgin wool from?
Ugly sheep.

Remember this one?

Customer: I'd like a pair of stockings for my wife.
  Storekeeper: Sheer?
  Customer: No, she's at home.

Q: Why was the pasty in the pub?
A: He was meetin' potato

Now we're getting somewhere

A policeman pulls over a car for swerving and asks the driver to take a breathalyzer test. "I can't do that," says the man. "I'm an asthmatic. The breathalyzer could bring on an attack."

So the policeman suggests a urine sample. "Can't do it," says the man. "I'm a diabetic, so my urine always has strange stuff in it."

"Well," says the angry policeman, "why don't you just get out of the car and walk along this white line?"

"Sorry," says the man, "but I can't do that either." "Why not?" asks the officer.

"Because I'm drunk."

Role model

Three young boys are trying to figure out whose dad is best.

"My dad is so good he can shoot an arrow, run after it, get in front of it, and catch it in his bare hands," says the first lad.

"My dad is so good that he can shoot a gun, run after the bullet, get in front of it and catch it in his bare hands," says the second lad.

"I've got you both beat," says the third lad. "My dad works for the council, and he's so good he can get off work at five and be home by 4:30!"

Patient: "Doctor, I've got a strawberry stuck up my bum."

Doctor: "I've got some cream for that."

That's why I don't believe in you

An atheist explorer in the deepest Amazon suddenly finds himself surrounded by a group of bloodthirsty natives. Upon surveying the situation, he says quietly to himself, "Oh, God. I'm screwed this time!"

There is a ray of light from Heaven and a voice booms out, "No, you are not screwed. All you have to do is pick up that stone at your feet and bash in the head of the chief standing in front of you."

So the explorer picks up the stone and proceeds to bash the chief until he's unconscious. As he stands above the body, breathing heavily and surrounded by hundreds of natives with looks of shock and anger on their faces, God's voice booms out again and says, "OK... now you're screwed."

Don't you just hate it when that happens?

A cowboy walks into a saloon and says, "Who painted my horse's balls yellow?"

Suddenly, a huge, mean-looking cowboy stands up and says, "I did."

So the first guy looks up at him and says, "Great. The first coat's dry."

There, but for the grace of God...

A man placed some flowers on the grave of his mother and was starting back towards his car when his attention was diverted to another man kneeling at a grave. The man kept repeating, "Why did you have to die?"

The first man approached him and said, "I don't wish to interfere with your private grief, but can I ask who you're mourning for?"

The mourner took a moment to collect himself, then replied, "My wife's first husband."

The other half

A man starts a new job, and his boss says, "If you marry my daughter, I'll make you a partner and give you a £1million salary."

The man's puzzled, until he sees a picture of the girl – she makes Margaret Thatcher look hot. But after a moment he accepts, figuring the money's worth it, and they get married.

A year later the fella's up on a ladder hanging a picture and yells to his wife, "Bring me my hammer, please."

She mumbles, "Get the hammer, get the hammer," and grudgingly fetches the hammer.

The guy says, "Can you hand me the nails, please?"

She mumbles, "Get me some nails, get me some nails," and does so.

The guy starts hammering, hits his thumb, and yells, "Ow! F**k me!"

She shuffles off, mumbling, "Get the bag, get the bag..."

What does a redneck always say just before he dies?
"Hey! Watch this."

Thanks for nothing

A woman's husband has been slipping in and out of a coma for several months, yet she stays lovingly by his bedside every day. Finally, he comes to and motions for her to come near. "You, my love," he says, "have been with me through all the bad times. When I was fired, you were there for me. When the business failed, you were there. When I got shot, you were by my side. When we lost the house, you stood by me throughout. When my health started failing, you were still by my side. You know what?" "What, dear?" she asks, gently. "I think you bring me bad luck."

Salesmanship

The flower vendor is an old hand at unloading his last few bunches each day. Appealing to a businessman on his way home, the vendor says, "How about a nice bunch of roses to surprise your wife?"

"Haven't got a wife," the businessman responds.

"Then how about some carnations for your girlfriend?" the vendor proposes without missing a beat.

"Haven't got a girlfriend."

The vendor breaks into a big smile. "Oh, then you'll want all the flowers I've got left. You have a lot to celebrate!"

Quick thinking

One fine spring day, a farmer walks through his orchard to a nearby pond, carrying a bucket of fruit. Once there, he spies two sexy young women skinny-dipping. Spotting him, they duck down below the water so that only their heads are visible.

"We're not coming out until you leave!" shouts one of the girls. Thinking on his feet, the farmer replies: "Oh, I'm not here to see you two – just here to feed the piranhas!"

Land that time forgot

After living in the remote wilderness of Norfolk all his life, an old man decides it's finally time to visit Norwich. In one of the shops he picks up a mirror and looks in it.

Not knowing what it is, he remarks, "How about that? Here's a picture of my dead daddy."

He buys the 'picture', but on the way home he remembers his wife, Lizzy, didn't like his father, so he hangs it in the barn, and every morning before leaving for the fields, he goes there to look at it. Lizzy begins to get suspicious of these many trips to the barn. One day after her husband leaves, she searches the barn and finds the mirror.

As she looks into the glass, she fumes, "So that's the ugly bitch he's runnin' around with…"

A lesson for life

Once upon a time, there lived an orphaned bunny and an orphaned snake who were both blind from birth. One day, the two met and decided to help one another out.

"Maybe I could slither all over you, and work out what you are," hissed the snake. "Oh, that would be wonderful," replied the bunny.

So the snake slithered all over the bunny, and said, "Well, you're covered with soft fur, your nose twitches, and you have a soft, cottony tail. I'd say that you must be a bunny rabbit."

The bunny then suggested to the snake, "Maybe I could feel you all over with my paw, and help you find out what you are." So the bunny felt the snake all over, and said, "Well, you're slippery, you have no backbone and no balls.

I'd say you must be either a team leader, supervisor or management."

How do you keep a kid from wetting the bed?
Give him an electric blanket.

Bird brain

A man follows a woman with a parrot out of a cinema, stops her and says, "I'm sorry to bother you, but I couldn't help noticing that your bird seemed to understand the film. He cried at the right parts, and he laughed at the jokes. Don't you find that unusual?"

"I do indeed," she replies. "He hated the book."

Wisdom of age

Three old men are at the hospital for a memory test. "What's three times three?" the doctor asks the first old man.

"Two hundred and seventy-four," he replies. "What's three times three?" the doctor asks the second old man. "Tuesday," he replies.

The doctor quickly realises he's in for a very long morning. He turns to the third old man and asks, "OK, your turn. What's three times three?" "Nine," he replies.

"Yes!" exclaims the doctor. "How did you get that?"

"Easy. I just subtracted 274 from Tuesday."

Life's little joke

Two men waiting at the Pearly Gates strike up a conversation.

"How'd you die?" the first man asks the second.

"I froze to death," says the second.

"That's awful," says the first man. "How does it feel to freeze to death?"

"It's very uncomfortable at first," says the second man. "You get the shakes, and you get pains in all your fingers and toes. But eventually, it's a very calm way to go. You get numb and you kind of drift off, as if you're sleeping. How about you, how did you die?"

"I had a heart attack," says the first man. "You see, I knew my wife was cheating on me, so one day I showed up at home unexpectedly. I ran up to the bedroom, and found her alone, knitting. I ran down to the basement, but no one was hiding there, either. I ran up to the second floor, but no one was hiding there either. I ran as fast as I could to the attic, and just as I got there, I had a massive heart attack and died."

The second man shakes his head. "That's so ironic," he says.

"What do you mean?" asks the first man.

"If you'd only stopped to look in the freezer, we'd both still be alive."

Easy, tiger

Some friends are playing a round of golf when they hear shouts in the distance. Looking across, they watch, amazed, as a buxom lady runs on to the fairway, pulls off some of her clothes and sprints up the course. Not two minutes later, two men in white coats appear and ask which way the woman has gone. They point up the course and the two men run off in that direction.

Bemused, the golfers carry on with their game, but are again disturbed by another man. This time he's staggering over the hill, panting with the effort of carrying two buckets of sand. Between wheezes, the newcomer too asks which way the woman has gone, and then totters away. Increasingly baffled, the golf party runs after the figure. "What the hell is going on?" they ask.

Gasping, the man explains. "That woman has escaped from our treatment clinic. She has acute nymphomania, and as soon as she gets all her clothes off, the nearest man is ravished."

"But why do you need two buckets of sand?" shout the golfers after him.

"Well, I caught her the last time she escaped," pants the man, "so it's my turn for the handicap."

Somebody's got to do it

A tourist in Egypt gets chatting to a man in a bar.

"What do you do for a living," asks the traveller.

"I'm a camel castrator," replies the Egyptian.

"Really? How do you go about castrating a camel?" asks the bewildered tourist.

"Well," says the man, "you go behind him and spread his legs. Then you take a big rock in each hand and smack his testicles between the rocks."

"Bugger me! That must hurt," asks the tourist.

"Not if you keep your thumbs out of the way."

Mary, Mary, quite contrary

What's the title of the Da Vinci Code film sequel?
   I Know What You Did Last Supper

What's the difference between worry and panic?
About 28 days.

Rules are rules

A brain and two turds go into a pub. The barman says to the brain, "I'm not serving you. Get out!" The brain asks why, and so the barman replies, "Because you're out of your head and your two mates are steaming!"

The joy of sex

After marrying a younger woman, a middle-aged man finds that no matter what he does in the sack, she never achieves orgasm. So he visits his doctor for advice. "Maybe fantasy is the solution," says the doctor. "Why not hire a strapping young man and, while you two are making love, have him wave a towel over you?"

The doctor smiles. "Make sure he's totally naked; that way your wife can fantasise her way to a full-blown orgasm."

Optimistic, he returns home and hires a handsome young escort. But it's no use; even when the stud stands naked, waving the towel, the wife remains unsatisfied. Perplexed, the man returns to his doctor.

"Try reversing it for a while," says the quack. "Have the young man make love to your wife and you wave the towel over them."

And so he returns home to try again, this time waving the towel as the same escort pumps away enthusiastically. Soon, the wife has an enormous, screaming orgasm. Smiling, the husband drops the towel and taps the young man on the shoulder.

"You see?" he shouts triumphantly. "That's how you wave a bloody towel."

I wink, therefore I am

A man with a winking problem applies for a position as a travelling sales rep and goes in for the interview.

"You're more than qualified," says the interviewer, "but we can't have our sales reps constantly winking at customers. We can't hire you."

"But wait," says the man. "If I take two aspirin, I stop winking."

"Show me," replies the interviewer.

The man then reaches into his pocket and pulls out a pile of condoms in all different shapes, sizes and colours before finally finding a packet of aspirin. He takes the pill and immediately stops winking.

"That's great," says the interviewer, "but we can't have our reps womanising all the time."

"I'm happily married," gasps the man.

"And the condoms?" asks the interviewer.

"Oh," sighs the man. "Well, have you ever tried walking into a chemist, winking and asking for aspirin?"

If that don't beat all...

Three cowboys are sitting in the bunkhouse. "That smart-arse Tex," says the first. "He's going to start bragging about that new foreign car he bought as soon as he comes in." "Not Tex," says the second. "He's just a good ol' boy. When he walks in, I'm sure all he'll say is, 'Hello'." "I know Tex better than any of you," says the third. "He's so smart, he'll figure out a way to do both. Here he comes now."

Tex then swings open the bunkhouse door and shouts, "Audi, partners!"

Child prodigy

Little Johnny returned home from school, informing his father that he'd received an F in maths and a detention.

"What happened?" asked his dad.

"Well," little Johnny said, "the teacher asked, 'How much is two times three?' and I said 'Six'."

"But that's right!" said his father.

"Then," said Johnny, "she asked, 'How much is three times two?'"

"That's crap. What's the difference?" asked his father.

"That's what I said!"

Dog food

One day, a little 5'1" guy walks into a pub and asks: "Excuse me; does anyone here own a big Rottweiler?"

A 7'1" man stands up and says: "That's Tyson. He's mine; why?"

"I think my dog has killed yours," says the pipsqueak, eyeing the big guy nervously.

"I don't believe it," says the hard lad. "What breed is your dog? Doberman? Pit Bull?"

"No, it's a Chihuahua," says the man.

"How can a Chihuahua kill a Rottweiler?" asks the owner.

"It got stuck in your dog's throat," replies the little fella.

> **"Knock, knock."**
> **"Who's there?"**
> **"Control freak. Now this is where you say, 'Control freak who?'"**

Little bastard!

Standing at a urinal, a man notices a midget is watching him. The man doesn't feel uncomfortable until the midget drags a small stepladder over to him, climbs it, and proceeds to admire his privates close up. "Wow!" says the little fella. "I bet you don't have any problem with the ladies."

Surprised and flattered, the man thanks the midget and starts to move away. But the little man stops him. "I know this is a strange request, but can I take a closer look?"

Before the man can stop him, the wee man reaches out and tightly grabs the man's testicles. "OK," he shouts. "Hand over your wallet or I'll jump."

Going too far

A shaven-headed Britney Spears goes to a psychiatrist to seek help.

"I don't know what to do," says the bald-headed pop princess. "My life's a complete mess."

The shrink looks over his glasses at her and says, "Your current antics are a cry for help, Miss Spears. After all you've been in the limelight most of your life, starting with the Mickey Mouse Club."

Suddenly, Spears stands up and shouts, "How dare you! I've never played for Arsenal!"

Marital relations

Mr Johnson and his secretary are on a first-class flight. As they're nodding off for the night, the secretary, who has long had a crush on her boss, says in her most seductive voice, "I'm a little cold. Can I get under your blanket?"

Reading her signals clearly, the boss says, "How would you like to be Mrs Johnson for a while?"

"I'd love it!" the secretary replies, jumping at the chance.

"Great," Mr Johnson says, "then get your own damn blanket."

Divine protection

Reggie Kray dies and goes to Heaven. At the Pearly Gates, Saint Peter asks his name.

"Kray. Reginald," he replies.

Saint Peter looks him up on the computer and it comes up on his database with a list of crimes as long as his arm.

Worried, Saint Peter goes to check with God before he can let him in.

"This is no good," says God. "Send him downstairs to Hell."

Saint Peter goes back out to the gates and says, "I'm sorry, Mr Kray, but we can't let you in." To which Reggie replies, "I don't want to come in. I want £2,000 a week or I'm shutting you down."

Ask a silly question

At 7am, a lone wife hears a key in the front door. She wanders down, bleary-eyed, to find her husband in the kitchen – drunk, with ruffled hair and lipstick on his collar. "I assume," she snarls, "that there's a very good reason for you to come waltzing in here at seven in the morning?"

"There is," he replies. "Breakfast."

Take me to your larder

What do you call a fat alien?

An extra-cholesterol.

How are politicians like nappies?

You have to change them frequently, and for the same reason.

Simple, Inuit?

1st Eskimo: Where did your mother come from?

2nd Eskimo: Alaska.

1st Eskimo: Don't bother; I'll ask her myself.

Why doesn't Mexico have an Olympic team?

Because everybody who can run, jump or swim is already in the US.

Johnny, remember me

A beautiful woman is driving back to the city when her sports car breaks down. Desperate, she wanders over the fields and spies a farmhouse where she knocks on the door.

"Oh, thank God", she says, when the farmer answers. "My car's broken down. Could I stay the night until someone comes out tomorrow?"

The farmer eyes her suspiciously. "Well, OK," he says "but don't mess with my two sons, Jed and Jake."

Behind him, two strapping young men appear, smiling sheepishly. The woman agrees, but after going to the guest room, she can't stop thinking about the two young bucks in the next room. Throwing caution to the wind, she quietly tip-toes across.

"Jake! Jed!" she whispers. "Would you like me to teach you the ways of the world?"

"Huh?" comes the reply.

"The only thing is I don't want to get pregnant – so you'll have to wear these condoms."

Beaming, the boys agree and soon embark on a glorious night of saucy three-way passion. Forty years later, Jed and Jake are sitting on their front porch, fondly remembering their erotic experience.

"It was fantastic, but I do have one question" says Jed.

"Oh?" says Jake .

His brother frowns, "Well, do you really care if the woman gets pregnant?"

"Nope" says Jake thoughtfully. "I reckon not."

"Me neither." says Jed. "Let's take these things off."

Suspicious minds

A worried man calls up his best mate in a panic. "I really need your advice, pal. I'm desperate and I don't know what to do."

His friend replies, "Sure, I'll try and help. What's wrong?" The worried man explains: "For some time now, I've suspected that my wife may be cheating on me. You know the sort of thing; the phone rings, I answer, someone hangs up."

"That's terrible, mate," says his friend.

"That's not all," continues the worried man. "The other day, I picked up her mobile, just to see what time it was, and she went mental, screaming at me that I should never touch her phone again, and that I was checking up on her. So far I haven't confronted her about it. I sort of think, deep down, I don't really want to know the truth. But then, last night, she went out again and I decided to check up on her. I hid bchind my car, which I knew would give me a good view of the whole street. That way, I could see which car she got out of on her return. Anyway, it was while I was crouched behind my car that I noticed some rust around the rear wheel arch. So, do you think I should take it into a body repair shop, or just buy some of that stuff from Halfords and try to sort it out myself?"

Lowest of the low

Why did God make snakes just before estate agents?
  To practice.

Unstoppable Turkey

What's the difference between bird flu and Man City? Bird flu has got to Europe.

Youth versus age

A young naval student is asked by an old sea captain: "What would you do if a sudden storm sprang up on the starboard?"
  "Throw out an anchor, sir," the student replies, promptly.
  "And what would you do if a storm sprang up aft?"
  "Throw out another anchor, sir," comes back the student. "And if another terrific storm sprang up forward, what would you do?" says the captain.
  "Throw out another anchor," replies the student. "Hold on," says the captain. "Where are you getting all your anchors from?"
  "Same place you're getting your storms, sir."

Mind your language

Little 10-year-old Freddie goes for a long weekend with his uncle, a wealthy Hampshire farm-owner. One evening, as Uncle John and his wife are entertaining guests with cocktails, they are interrupted by an out-of-breath Freddie who shouts out, "Uncle John! Come quick! The bull is f**king the cow!"

Uncle John, highly embarrassed, takes young Freddie aside, and explains that a certain amount of decorum is required. "You should have said, 'The bull is surprising the cow' – not some filth picked up in the playground," he says.

A few days later, Freddie comes in again as his aunt and uncle are entertaining guests. "Uncle John! The bull is surprising the cows!"

The adults share a knowing grin.

Uncle John says, "Thank you Freddie, but surely you meant to say the cow, not cows. A bull cannot surprise more than one cow at a time, you know..."

"Yes, he can!" replies his nephew. "He's f**king the horse!"

Your call

A husband and wife are watching *Who Wants To Be A Millionaire?* It gets the husband thinking and he looks over at his wife, winks and says, "Honey, let's go upstairs."

"No," sighs his wife.

The husband looks at her and says, "Is that your final answer?"

"Yes," she replies.

"In that case," smiles hubby, "can I phone a friend?"

What makes men chase women they have no intention of marrying?
The same urge that makes dogs chase cars they have no intention of driving.

Raise your glasses

A man walks into a pub, sits down, orders three pints of lager, drinks them and then leaves. This continues daily for several weeks.

Curious, the pub landlord approaches him one day. "Why do you always order three pints of lager?" he asks. "Well," says the man, "my two brothers and I always used to have a pint each and since they've both passed on, I've continued to order the three beers in their honour." The landlord is taken aback by such nobility and welcomes the man whenever he then visits the pub. But two weeks later, the man strolls in and orders not his usual three pints, but only two. Surprised, the landlord asks what the problem is. "Oh, no problem at all," smiles the man. "I've just decided to stop drinking."

Getting his backup

Jesus and Satan are having an ongoing argument about who's better on their computer. Finally, God says, "I am going to set up a test which will take two hours and I will judge who does the better job."

So Satan and Jesus sit down at the keyboards and type away. They do everything their PCs can handle. But, ten minutes before the time's up, lightning suddenly flashes across the sky, and the electricity goes off.

Satan stares at his blank screen and screams in every curse word known in the underworld. Jesus just sighs. The electricity finally flickers back on, and each of them reboots.

Satan starts searching, frantically screaming, "It's gone! It's all gone! I lost everything when the power went out!"

Meanwhile, Jesus quietly starts printing out all his files from the past two hours. Satan sees this and becomes even more irate. "Wait! He cheated! How did he do it!?"

God shrugs and says, "Jesus saves."

Freezer jolly good fellow

70-year-old George goes for his annual check-up. He tells the doctor that he feels fine, but often has to go to the bathroom during the night. Then he says: "But you know, Doc: I'm blessed. God knows my eyesight is going, so he puts on the light when I pee, and turns it off when I'm done!"

A little later in the day, Dr. Smith calls George's wife and says: "Your husband's test results were fine, but he said something strange that has been bugging me. He claims that God turns the light on and off for him when he uses the bathroom at night."

Thelma exclaims: "That old fool! He's been peeing in the refrigerator again!"

Last rites

A priest is preparing a man for his passing over. Whispering firmly, the priest says, "Denounce the devil! Let him know how little you think of him!"

The dying man says nothing. The priest repeats his order. Still the man says nothing.

The priest asks, "Why do you refuse to denounce the devil and his evil?"

The dying man replies, "Until I know for sure where I'm headed, I don't think I ought to aggravate anybody."

Chop, chop!

A man sticks his head into a hairdresser's and asks, "How long is the wait?"

"About two hours," the barber says, and the man leaves.

A few days later, the same man pokes his head in and again asks, "How long is the wait?"

"About two hours," the barber replies. The guy leaves again. A week later, the man pops in and asks the same question. The barber replies, "About an hour."

Once again, the man leaves, but this time the barber sends his friend to follow the man.

His mate returns later, looking sheepish. "So where does he go after leaving my shop?" the barber asks.

"Your house," his mate replies.

What do you call a randy dwarf?
A low blow.

Salt and vinegar?

A man goes into a fish and chip shop and says "Can I have fish and chips twice, please?"

The shop owner says, "I heard you the first time."

Taking the Mickey

Why did Euro Disney have to close down?

Health and Safety found a five-foot mouse in the restaurant.

Wonders of modern technology

A man walks into a pub, orders a beer and begins punching his hand with his finger as if he was dialling a phone.

"What are you doing, mate?" asks the very curious landlord.

"I've had a phone installed in my hand because I was tired of carrying one around," the man answers. "Try it!"

The man dials a number and puts his hand up to the landlord's ear. The owner of the pub across the street picks up and the landlord can't believe it.

"Amazing, eh?" says the man. "Now, where's the gents?" The landlord tells him, but when the man doesn't come back for over an hour, the landlord goes looking for him.

He finds him in the gents, spread-eagled against the wall with his trousers around his ankles and a roll of toilet paper coming out of his underpants.

"My God!" the landlord yells. "Were you mugged?"

The man turns to him and says, "No, I'm fine. Just waiting for a fax."

Mysterious ways

A drunken priest is pulled over for speeding. Smelling alcohol on the father's breath and noticing a wine bottle on the passenger seat, the copper asks, "Sir, have you been drinking?"

The minister replies, "Just water."

"Then tell me," the policeman enquires.

"How is it that I can smell wine?"

The minister looks down at the bottle and exclaims, "Good Lord, He's done it again!"

Nuts

Delicate matter

A newlywed couple arrive back from their honeymoon to move into their tiny new flat.

"Care to go to bed?" the husband asks.

"Shh!" says his blushing bride. "These walls are paper-thin; the neighbours will know what you mean! Next time, ask me in code, like: 'Have you left the washing machine door open?' instead."

So, the following night, the husband asks: "I don't suppose you left the washing machine door open, darling?"

"No," she snaps back, "I definitely shut it." Then she rolls over and falls asleep.

The next morning, she wakes up feeling a little frisky herself, so she nudges her husband and says: "I think I did leave the washing machine door open after all..."

"Don't worry," says the man. "It was only a small load, so I did it by hand."

Gallant allies

During WW II an American soldier has been on the front line in Europe for three months, when he is finally given a week of R & R. He catches a supply boat to a base in the south of England, and then catches a train to London. The train is extremely crowded and he can't find a seat. He is dead on his feet and walks the length of the train looking for any place to sit down. Finally he finds a compartment with seats facing each other; there is room for two people on each seat. On one side sits a proper-looking, older British lady with a small dog sitting in the empty seat beside her.

"Could I please sit in that seat?" asks the Yank.

The lady is insulted. "You bloody Americans are so rude," she says. "Can't you see my dog is sitting there?"

"Lady, I love dogs," says the American. "I have a couple at home – so I would be glad to hold your dog if I could sit down."

The lady replies, "You Americans are not only rude; you are arrogant too."

He leans against the wall for a time, but is so tired he finally says, "Lady, I've been on the front line in Europe for three months with not a decent rest for all that time. Could I please sit there and hold your dog?"

The lady replies, "You Americans are not only rude and arrogant; you are also obnoxious!"

With that comment, the soldier calmly steps in, picks up the dog, throws it out the window, and sits down. The lady is speechless.

An older, neatly-dressed Englishman sitting across on the other seat suddenly says, "Young man, I do not know if all you Americans fit the lady's description of you or not: but I do know that you Americans do a lot of things wrong. You drive on the wrong side of the road, you hold your fork with the wrong hand, and now you have just thrown the wrong bitch out of the window."

What's the difference between dogs and foxes?
About four pints.

Vegging out

A guy walks into a watchmaker's shop and asks the man
behind the counter for a potato clock.

"A potato clock?" says the watchmaker, "I've never heard of
a potato clock. Why do you want one?"

The customer sighs. "Well, you see," he says, "I went
for a job interview yesterday and was offered the job. So I
asked the boss what time I should start, and he said nine
o'clock."

"So?" asks the kindly old shopkeeper.

"Well," replies the man, "he said to do that, I'll need to get a
potato clock."

Keeping up appearances

A man weds his virgin bride and on the big night, strips off
and jumps into bed for a grope. Taken aback, his new wife lays
down the law. "I expect you to be as well-mannered in bed as
you are at the dinner table, my love!"

"Oh right," says the man, backing off a bit. "Well, then, will
you please pass the sex?"

Playing the game

A man walks up to a woman and asks, "Would you sleep with
me for £1,000,000?"

She quickly replies, "Yes."

So then he asks, "Would you sleep with me for £20?"

Astounded by the question, she says, "Of course not. What kind of woman do you think I am?"

He says, "Well, we've already determined that. Now I'm just working on a price."

Fashion victim

David Beckham is walking through the jungle with Posh when he suddenly turns to her and says, "Look at that flash bastard with the all-in-one Lacoste sleeping bag."

Not right in the head

A woman goes to see her GP about something that has been troubling her for some time.

"Doctor, I keep thinking I'm a cartoon character," she says. "One day it's Mickey Mouse, the next it's Donald Duck. This morning I woke up and I was convinced I was Bambi."

"Well," replies the Doc. "It just sounds to me like you're having Disney spells."

What do you get when you mix a
laxative with holy water?
A religious movement.

Game of skill

The owner of a petrol station tries to boost sales by posting a
sign that says, "Free sex with every fill-up." Before long, two
rednecks pull in. The driver gets out, fills his tank and then
enquires about the offer.

"Pick a number between one and ten," says the owner. "If
you guess correctly, you win free sex!" The customer thinks for
a bit, then finally guesses eight. "No, but you were really close,"
smiles the owner. "The actual number was seven. Better luck
next time, eh?"

As the two men pull away, the driver says to his mate, "You
know what, I reckon that game was rigged. I bet you he doesn't
really give away free sex at all."

"Oh no, it ain't rigged," replies his mate. "My wife won three
times last week..."

Going bananas

A gorilla walks into a bar and orders a pint of lager. The
barman charges him five quid and, after looking at him for a
while, says, "Do you know, you're the first gorilla we've had in
here for ages?"

"I'm not bloody surprised," replies the gorilla, "at a fiver a
pint."

Signs of stress

A psychology tutor is giving her class an oral test on mental health. Singling out a student, she grills him on manic depression: "How would you diagnose a patient who walks back and forth screaming at the top of his lungs one minute, then sits in a chair weeping uncontrollably the next?"

The young man thinks for a moment, then offers his answer: "Premiership manager?"

About to snap

A photographer for a national magazine is assigned to get photos of a great forest fire. Smoke at the scene is too thick to get any good shots, so he frantically calls his office to hire a plane.

"It will be waiting for you at the airport!" he is assured by his editor. As soon as he gets to the small, rural airport, sure enough, a plane is warming up near the runway. He jumps in with his equipment and yells, "Let's go! Let's go!" The pilot swings the plane into the wind and soon they are airborne.

"Fly over the north side of the fire," says the photographer, "and make three or four low-level passes."

"Why?" asks the pilot.

"Because I'm going to take pictures! I'm a photographer, and photographers take pictures!" says the photographer with great exasperation.

After a long gulp, the pilot says, "You mean you're not the instructor?"

Oh, God

A burglar breaks into a house and creeps into a room with no lights on. He walks into the room and hears a voice which says, "Jesus is watching you."

The thief turns around and, in a dark corner of the room, he sees a parrot. As he creeps over to shut the bird up, the parrot shrieks again, "Jesus is watching you."

The annoyed burglar looks at the parrot and asks, "What's your name?" The parrot replies, "Clarence."

The burglar laughs and, as he's about to throttle the bird, says, "That's a stupid name for a parrot. What idiot called you that?"

The parrot replies, "The same idiot who decided to call the rottweiler Jesus."

Funny because it's true

What's six inches long, with a head on it, that women like to blow?

Money.

White man speak with forked tongue

The Lone Ranger is riding through the mountains when Indians attack. They drag him from his horse and bury him in the sand up to his neck, ready to kill him. Knowing he's about to kick the bucket, the Lone Ranger calls his horse over and whispers in his ear. The horse gallops off and returns a few minutes later with a gorgeous naked blonde girl on its back.

After surveying the scene she hops down out of the saddle and sits on his face, sighing and moaning as she writhes about. When she's finished the Indians dive in for the kill.

"Stop! I just want one more word with my horse," cries the Lone Ranger.

They agree and his steed trots over to hear his final words.

"I said 'Posse', you useless tw*t!"

What are the three main food groups?
Fast, frozen and instant.

A short life, but a merry one

A man bursts into a busy pub, points to his left and shouts, "All the arseholes over that side!" He then points to his right and shouts, "All the dickheads get over that side!"

Suddenly, the hardest guy in the pub stands up and says, "Who are you calling a dickhead?"

The man points to his left and shouts, "Over there, arsehole!"

If you must

A man is pleasuring a lady. "Would you like to try the social security position?" he asks her.

"What on earth is that?" she replies. "Well," explains the man, "when my balls are touching your arse, you're getting full benefit!"

Personal services

A man is sitting at a bar enjoying a drink when an exceptionally gorgeous young woman walks in. The man can't take his eyes off her. Noticing his overly attentive stare, she walks directly over to him and, before he can even apologise for gawping, she makes him an offer: "I'll do absolutely anything you want me to, no matter how kinky it is, for £100. However, there is one condition..."

Naturally, the man asks what the condition is. "Well," says the woman, "you have to tell me what you want me to do in three words."

The man considers the proposition for a moment, takes out his wallet and slowly counts out five £20 notes. He presses each note into the young woman's hand, looks excitedly into her eyes and finally says: "Paint my house."

It brings it all back

A local reporter goes to an old people's home to interview an ageing but legendary explorer. After hearing many incredible tales, he asks the old man to tell him about the most frightening experience he ever had on his travels. "Once, I was hunting tigers in the jungles of India. I was on a narrow path and my native guide was behind me, carrying my rifle. Just then, the largest tiger I've ever seen leapt out in front of us. I turned around for my weapon only to find that the native had fled. The tiger pounced at me with a mighty 'Roarrrr!' I'm sorry to say I soiled myself."

The reporter says, "Sir, don't be embarrassed. Under those circumstances anyone would have done the same." "No, not then," the old man replies. "Just now, when I went 'Roarrrr!'"

Old retainer

A man was passing a country estate and saw a sign on the gate. It read: "Please ring bell for the caretaker." He rang the bell and an old man appeared.

"Are you the caretaker?" the fellow asked.

"Yes, I am," replied the old man. "What do you want?"

"I'd just like to know why you can't ring the bell yourself."

It's an ill wind...

James Blunt, Westlife, Justin Timberlake and the Pussycat Dolls are on a sinking ship. Who gets saved?

The world of music.

Necessary evil

An Amish woman is driving her horse and buggy down the
road when she gets pulled over.

"You have a broken reflector on your buggy," the policeman
says, "but more important, one of your reins is looped around
your horse's balls. That's cruelty to animals. Have your
husband take care of that right away!"

Later that day, the woman tells her husband, "A policeman
pulled me over today for two reasons. First, he said the
reflector was broken."

"Well, that's easily fixed," says her husband. "What else?"

"I'm not sure: something about the emergency brake."

**What do you do with a three-legged
dog?**
Take it for a drag.

And justice for all

On trial in a rural American town, an English man thinks he
has no chance of getting off a murder charge, despite his
innocence. So, shortly before the jury retires, he bribes one of
the jurors to find him guilty of the lesser crime of manslaughter.

The jury is out for over three days before eventually
returning a verdict of manslaughter.

The relieved defendant collars the bribed juror and says:
"Thanks. However did you manage it?"

"It wasn't easy," admits the juror. "All the others wanted to acquit you."

Doctor's dilemma

An 85-year-old man goes to his doctor's to get a sperm count.

The doctor gives him a jar and says: "Take this jar home and bring back a semen sample tomorrow."

The next day the old boy reappears at the doctor's office and gives him the jar, which is as clean and empty as on the previous day. The doctor asks what happened and the man explains: "Well, doc, it's like this; first I tried with my right hand, but nothing. Then I tried with my left hand, but still nothing. Then I asked my wife for help. She tried with her right hand, her left, with her mouth, first with the teeth in, then with her teeth out and still nothing. We even called up Arlene, our neighbour, and she tried too, with both hands, then an armpit and she even tried squeezing it between her knees, but still nothing."

The doctor is shocked. "You asked your neighbour?"

The old man replies, "Yep. And no matter what we tried, we still couldn't get the jar open."

Crime against humanity

An accordionist is driving home from a late-night gig. Feeling tired, he pulls into a service station for some coffee. While waiting to pay, he remembers that he locked his car doors but left the accordion in plain view on the back seat of his car! He rushes out only to realise that he is too late. The back window of his car has been smashed and somebody's already thrown in two more accordions.

Kill yourself now

A man has huge feet. Wherever he goes, people take the mick.
Sitting on the beach wall with his plates dangling in the water,
a vicar strolls past and can see the man is upset, so he walks
over and asks, "What's the matter?"

"I'm so depressed," replies the man. "Everywhere I go,
people ridicule me for the size of my feet."

The vicar comes up with a plan and tells the man, "Dye your
hair a brilliant green and, that way, people will look at your
hair and not your feet!"

The man thanks the vicar for the advice, goes to the nearest
hair salon and has his hair dyed. He walks out feeling fantastic
– better than he's felt in a long time. He bounds down the road
and a passer-by shouts out, "Hey, you with the green hair!"

He turns around and shouts confidently back, "Yeah?" "Ha,
ha," laughs the passer-by. "You've got bloody massive feet, mate!"

Rotten to macaw

A woman's dishwasher breaks down, so she calls a repairman.
Since she has to go to work the next day, she tells the
repairman, "I'll leave the key under the mat. Fix the
dishwasher, leave the bill on the counter, and I'll send you a
cheque in the post. Oh, by the way; don't worry about my
bulldog. He won't bother you. But, whatever you do, do not,
under any circumstances, talk to my parrot! I repeat, do not
talk to my parrot!"

When the repairman arrives at the woman's apartment the
following day, he discovers the biggest, meanest-looking bulldog
he has ever seen. But, just as the woman warns, the dog just

lays there on the carpet watching the repairman go about his work. The parrot, however, is driving the man nuts the whole time with his incessant yelling, cursing and name-calling.

Finally the repairman can contain himself no longer and yells, "Shut up, you stupid ugly bird!"

The parrot replies, "Get him, Spike."

> **There are two grains of sand in the desert.**
> **One turns to the other and says, "Busy here, isn't it?"**

Fishy business

A man calls home to his wife and says, "Honey, I've been asked to go fishing with my boss and several of his friends. We'll be gone for a week. This is a good opportunity for me to get that promotion I've been wanting. We're leaving from the office and I'll swing by the house to pick my things up. Oh – please pack my new blue silk pyjamas."

The wife thinks this sounds a little suspicious but being a good wife she does exactly what her husband asked. The following weekend he comes home a little tired but otherwise looking good.

The wife welcomes him home and asks if he caught many fish.

He says, "Loads! But why didn't you pack my new blue silk pyjamas like I asked you to do?"

The wife replies, "I did. They were in your tackle box..."

Give and take

Four blokes are making the most of a fine Sunday with a round of golf. During the fourth hole they discuss how they actually got away from their wives for the day.

First bloke: "You have no idea what I had to do to be able to come out golfing this weekend. I had to promise my wife that I'll paint every room in the house next weekend."

Second bloke: "That's nothing, I had to promise my wife that I'd build her a new deck for the pool."

Third bloke: "Man, you both have it easy! I had to promise my wife that I'd remodel the kitchen for her."

They continue to play the hole when they realized that the fourth bloke hasn't said a word. So they ask him. "You haven't said anything about what you had to do to be able to come golfing this weekend. What's the deal?"

The fourth bloke replies: "I just set my alarm for 5:30 am. When it goes off I give the wife a nudge and say, 'Golf course or intercourse?' So she says: 'Remember to wear your sweater, dear'."

What a way to go

How did the redneck die drinking milk?

The cow sat on him.

Countrymen

Tony Blair calls John Prescott into his office and says, "John, I have a great idea! We are going to go all-out to win back rural Britain."

"Great idea, Tony," says Prezza. "How will we go about it?"

"Well," says Blair, "we'll get ourselves tweed jackets, some

138

wellies, a stick, a flat cap and a Labrador. Then we'll really look the part. We'll go to a nice old country pub, in one of those posh villages, and we'll prove we really enjoy the countryside."

"Right," says Prescott.

So a few days later, all kitted out and with the requisite Labrador at heel, they set off from London in a westerly direction. Eventually they find a lovely country pub and go up to the bar.

"Good evening landlord, may we have two pints of your best ale?" says Blair.

"Good evening, Prime Minister," says the landlord, "two pints of best it is, coming up."

Blair and Prescott stand by the bar drinking their beer and chatting, nodding now and again to those who come in for a drink.

The dog lies quietly at their feet when, all of a sudden, the door from the adjacent bar opens and in walks an old shepherd, complete with crook. He goes up to the Labrador, lifts its tail and looks underneath, shrugs his shoulders and walks back to the other bar. Moments later, another old shepherd comes in with his crook and repeats what the first shepherd did before scratching his head and going back to the other bar. Over the course of the next half hour or so several other locals come in, lift the dog's tail and go away looking puzzled. Eventually Blair and Prescott can stand it no longer and call the landlord over.

"Tell me," says Blair. "Why do all these old shepherds and locals come in and look under the dog's tail like that? Is it a local custom?"

"Good Lord, no," says the landlord. "It's just that word spread to the other bar that there was a Labrador in this bar with two arseholes."

Best of friends

Spotting a monkey at the side of the road, a truck driver pulls over, opens the passenger door and asks, "Do you need a lift?"

The monkey hops in but, as they drive off, a policeman pulls them over.

"I want you to take that monkey to the zoo," the officer barks.

"Yeah, I suppose that would be the best thing to do with him," the truck driver agrees.

The next day, the policeman sees the monkey sitting in the same truck. So, he pulls the trucker over again and says, "I thought I told you to take that monkey to the zoo!"

The trucker replies, "Oh, I did, officer, and we had a great time. Today we're going fishing."

What goes "Oooooooooooo"?
A cow with no lips.

Well, when you put it like that...

A motorist screeches to a halt on a garage forecourt, looking for the man who sold him his car.

"Oi!" he shouts at a salesman. "I want a bloody word with you."

"What's the matter, sir?" says the salesman. "Everything OK with your car?"

"No, everything is not OK with my car. I bought this heap on the understanding that it was going to give me good performance and it'll only get to 110 uphill. It's ridiculous."

Taken aback, the salesman says, "Well, excuse me, sir, but I must point out that 110 uphill is very impressive for a car in this class."

"Impressive?" the man yells. "Not when I live at 136 it's not!"

Like father, like son

A little boy was lost in the supermarket. He went up to the security guard and said: "I've lost my dad."

The security guard asked him "What's he like?"

The little boy replied "Beer, kebabs and big tits."

National disgrace

What's the difference between OJ Simpson and the England football team?

OJ Simpson had a more credible defence.

So long, suckers!

A tour bus driver is driving a bus full of OAPs on holiday when a little old lady taps him on his shoulder. She offers him a handful of almonds, which he gratefully munches down. After about 15 minutes, she taps him on his shoulder again and she hands him another handful of almonds. She repeats this gesture about eight times. At the ninth time, he asks the little old lady why they don't eat the almonds themselves? She explains that because of their false teeth, they can't chew them.

"Why do you buy them then?" the puzzled driver asks. The old lady answers, "We just love the chocolate around them."

Human race

How do historians know the Indians were the first people in America?

They've seen their reservations.

Try, try again

In Jerusalem, a female CNN journalist hears about a very old Jewish man who has been going to the Wailing Wall to pray, twice a day, every day for years. So she goes to check it out. She walks to the Wailing Wall and there he is walking slowly up to the holy site. She watches him pray and after about 45 minutes, when he turns to leave, she approaches him for an interview.

"I'm Rebecca Smith from CNN. Sir, how long have you been coming to the Wailing Wall and praying?" she begins.

"For about 60 years," says the old fella.

"60 years! That's amazing! What do you pray for?"

"I pray for peace between the Muslims and the Jews. I pray for all the hatred to stop and I pray for all our children to grow up in safety and friendship," says the wizened old gent.

"How do you feel after doing this for 60 years?"

"Like I'm talking to a brick wall."

Mustn't grumble

Morris and his wife, Esther, went to the funfair every year. And every year, Morris would say, "Esther, I'd like to ride in that helicopter."

Esther always replied, "Yes, it looks fun, Morris, but that helicopter ride is £50 – and £50 is £50."

One year later, Esther and Morris went to the fair again. Morris said, "Esther, I'm 85 years old. If I don't ride that helicopter now, I might never get another chance."

Esther replied, "That's all very well, Morris, but that helicopter ride is £50 – and £50 is £50." The pilot overheard the couple. He said, "Folks, I'll make you a deal. I'll take both of you for a ride. If you can stay quiet for the entire ride and not say a word, I won't charge you. But if you say one word, it's £50."

Morris and Esther agreed and up they went. The pilot did all kinds of fancy manoeuvres, but not a word was heard. He did his daredevil tricks over and over again, but still not a word. When they landed, the pilot turned to Morris and said, "Blimey! I did everything I could to get you to yell out, but you didn't. I'm impressed!" Morris replied, "Well, I was going to say something when Esther fell out halfway through, but £50 is £50."

**What is a man's view of safe sex?
A padded headboard.**

Moving traffic violation

A man was pulled over by the police one day because his car didn't have any hubcaps on his tyres.

"What's the charge, officer?" asked the man.

The cop replied, "Indecent exposure."

"Indecent exposure!" exclaimed the fella.

The cop responded, "Yes! You can't just ride around with your nuts showing!"

Beyond the pale

A retiring golf club president is making his final speech at his club's annual awards ceremony. "From 18-handicappers to pros, I've treated everyone equally," the emotional president begins. "We all live for this game. We're like a big family and after all these years together I only fell by the wayside once.

While my darling wife sits beside me, I want to apologise to her and you, my beloved friends. In a mere moment of weakness, I betrayed her. It meant nothing – a one-night stand, that's all."

After this shocking revelation, the president sits down, ashamed. His wife rises, smiling as ever. "I, too, have a confession, darling," she says. "Before I met you, I was a man!" There are gasps around the room as the startled president staggers back to his feet. "You cheating bastard!" he exclaims. "All these years you played off the front tees."

A keen eye

A man applies for a job in a Florida lemon grove but seems to have no experience whatsoever.

The foreman is puzzled and asks the man, "I'm not sure that I can employ you because you just don't have the experience. Have you ever picked lots of lemons before?"

At this the man gets up and shouts, "What are you talking about? Don't you recognise me? I'm Gareth Southgate! I manage Middlesbrough!"

All right, you asked for it!

A primary school teacher was trying to get her class to stop speaking in 'baby talk' and insisted on 'big people' words only. She asked Chris what he had done over the weekend. "I visited my nana, Miss," said Chris.

"No, you went to visit your grandmother. We're using 'big people' words here, Chris!" She then asked Rupert what he had done.

"I took a ride on a choo-choo, Miss," replied Rupert. The teacher said, "No, Rupert, you took a ride on a train. You must remember to use 'big people' words."

She then asked little Alex what he had done.

"I read a book, Miss," he replied. "That's wonderful!" the teacher said. "What book did you read?" Alex thought for a second, before saying, "*Winnie the Shit*, Miss."

The birds and the bees

Two boys get their grades from their female sex education teacher. One gets a D and the other an F.

"We should get her for this," says the first boy.

"Yeah," the second agrees. "I'm going to kick her right in the nuts."

Well, whaddaya know?

A man was on holiday in Kenya. While he was walking through the bush, he came across an elephant standing with one leg raised in the air. The elephant seemed distressed, so the man approached it, very carefully. He got down on one knee and inspected the elephant's foot. There was a large thorn deeply embedded in the bottom of the foot. As carefully and as gently as he could he removed the thorn, and the elephant gingerly put down its foot. The elephant turned to face the man and with a rather stern look on its face, stared at him.

For a good ten minutes the man stood frozen, thinking of nothing else but being trampled. Eventually the wrinkly-skinned mammal trumpeted loudly, turned and walked away.

Years later, the man was walking through the zoo with his son. As they approached the elephant enclosure, one of the creatures turned and walked over to where they were standing at the rail. It stared at him, and the man couldn't help wondering if this was the same elephant. After a while it trumpeted loudly, then it continued to stare at him. The man summoned up his courage, climbed over the railing and made his way into the enclosure. He walked right up to the elephant and stared back in wonder. Suddenly the elephant trumpeted again, wrapped its trunk around one of the man's legs and swung him wildly back and forth along the railing, killing him.

Probably wasn't the same elephant.

Why do bagpipers walk when they play?
To get away from the sound.

The truth will out

A mum is driving her little girl to a friend's house to play.

"Mummy," the little girl asks. "How old are you?"

"You aren't supposed to ask a lady her age," the mother warns. "It's personal and it is not polite."

"OK," the little girl says. "Why did you and Daddy get a divorce?"

"That's enough questions. Honestly!" exclaims the exasperated mother, before walking away as the two friends begin to play.

"My mum wouldn't tell me anything," the little girl says to her friend.

"Well," said the friend. "All you need to do is look at her birth certificate. It has everything on it."

Later that night, the little girl says to her mother, "I know how old you are. You're 32."

The mother is surprised and asks, "How did you find that out?"

"And," the little girl says, triumphantly, "I know why you and Daddy got a divorce."

"Oh, really?" the mother asks, somewhat surprised. "And why's that?"

"Because you only got an F in sex."

Spit and polish

Pinocchio moaned to Gepetto that when he made love to his girlfriend she complained about splinters.

"Try some sandpaper, Pinocchio," advised Gepetto.

A month later Gepetto asked, "How's your love life, then? Is your girlfriend still complaining of splinters?"

"Who needs a girlfriend?" replied Pinocchio.

One liner

A wee Scottish man has worked in the Clyde shipyards all his life. He wins the lottery and decides to take his wife on a trip on one of the ships he helped build – the QE2. As it's a once-in-a-lifetime event, he goes the whole hog and takes one of the best rooms. Naturally, the captain hears one of the men who built the QE2 is on board, and the couple are invited to the captain's table at dinner.

The couple is sat next to an immensely wealthy lady at dinner who asks: "Have you sailed on the ship many times before?"

"Naw," says the Scottish fella's wife, "This is oor furst time!"

"Oh, I see," drawls the lady. "My husband and I make this trip three times every year."

"Three times? Every year?" squeaks the wee worker's wife, "how d'ye manage it?"

The lady coughs politely and says, "My husband works for Cunard, you know."

"Weell!" spits out the Scottish woman, "Mah man works f*ckin hard tae, but we don't brag aboot it!"

That sinking feeling

Three men are walking through the jungle when a native tribe ambushes them. The leader of the tribe offers each man one last request before being killed for trespassing. The first man asks for a big feast, so the tribe give him their best food and when he's full, they chop off his head.

"We shall make him into a canoe!" the leader exclaims.

The next man pleads to have sex one last time, so the tribe gets their sexiest woman and he has the best sex of his life.

Then the tribe chop off his head and again the leader says, "We shall make him into a canoe!"

The last man thinks for a second, then requests a fork. The tribe look confused, but give him a fork. Then the man starts to stab himself all over and shouts, "You're not making a bloody canoe out of me!"

How do you make a dog drink?
Put it in the liquidizer.

Bungle in the jungle

One fine day in the forest, Mr Rabbit is on his daily run when he sees a giraffe rolling a joint.

"Oh, Mr Giraffe!" he calls. "Why do you do drugs? Come run with me instead!" So the giraffe stops rolling and runs with the rabbit.

Then they come across an elephant doing lines of cocaine.

"Oh, Mr Elephant, why do you do drugs? Come run with us instead." So the elephant stops snorting, and goes running with the other two animals.

Then they spy a lion preparing a syringe. "Oh, Mr Lion," cries the rabbit, "why do you do drugs? Come run with us instead."

But no – with a mighty roar, the lion smashes the rabbit to smithereens. "No!" cry the giraffe and elephant. "Why did you do that? All he was trying to do was help you out!"

The lion growls. "That rabbit always makes me run around the forest when he's whizzing his tits off."

Ding-dong!

Upon hearing that her elderly grandfather had just passed away, Kate went to her grandparents' house to visit her 95-year-old grandmother.

When she asked how her grandfather had died, her grandmother replied, "He had a heart attack while we were making love on Sunday morning." Horrified, the woman told her grandmother that two people nearly 100 years old having sex would surely be asking for trouble.

"Oh no, my dear," replied Granny. "Many years ago, we figured out that the best time to do it was when the church bells started to ring. It was just the right rhythm – nice and slow and even. Nothing too strenuous for us." She paused to wipe away a tear, and continued, "He'd still be alive if the ice-cream van hadn't come along."

Advance planning

After fifty years of marriage to Lena, Ole becomes very ill and realises that he will soon die. In bed one night, Ole turns to his wife.

"Lena," he asks. "When I am gone, do you think you will marry another man?"

Lena gives it some thought. "Well, yes," she says. "Marriage has been good to me and I think that I will surely marry again."

Ole is taken aback. "Why, Lena," he cries, "will you bring your new husband into our house?"

"This is a fine house," says Lena. "Yes, I think we will live here."

"But Lena," Ole gasps, "will you bring your new husband into our bed?"

Lena replies, "Well, yes; you made this bed, a good strong bed. Yes! Sure I will bring my new husband into this bed."

Ole gulps. "But Lena," he says in a quiet voice. "You won't let your new husband use my golf clubs, will you?"

Lena smiled at her husband. "Oh, Ole!" she grins, misty-eyed. "Of course he won't use your golf clubs! He's left-handed."

A small kindness

One afternoon, a wealthy lawyer is riding in the back of his limousine when he sees two men eating grass by the roadside. He orders his driver to stop and he gets out to investigate.

"Why are you eating grass?" he asks one man.

"We don't have any money for food," the poor man replies.

"Oh, come along with me then."

"But sir, I have a wife with two children!"

"Bring them along! And you, come with us too!" he says to the other man.

"But sir, I have a wife with six children!" the second man answers.

"Bring them as well!"

They all climb into the car, which was no easy task, even for a car as large as the limo. Once under way, one of the poor fellows says, "Sir, you are too kind. Thank you for taking all of us with you."

The lawyer replies, "No problem; the grass at my home is about two feet tall!

The inevitable duck/pub joke

A duck walks into a bar and orders a pint of beer.

Amazed, the bartender says, "Hey, you can talk!"

"Sure, pal," says the duck. "Now can I get that drink?"

Shaking his head, the barman serves the duck a pint and asks him what he's doing in the area.

"I work on the building site across the street," says the duck.

"You should join the circus," says the barman. "You could make a mint."

"The circus?" the duck replies. "What the hell would the circus want with a bricklayer?"

How do you know if a stoner's crashed into your house?
He's still there.

Crap presents

Young Justin has a swearing problem, and his father's getting tired of it.

He decides to ask a shrink what to do. The shrink says, "Negative reinforcement. Since Christmas is coming up, ask Justin what he wants from Santa. If he swears while he tells you his wish list, leave a pile of dog poop in place of each gift he requests."

Two days before Christmas, Justin's father asks him what he wants for Christmas. "I want a damn teddy bear lying beside me when I wake up. When I go downstairs, I want to see a damn train going around the damn tree. And when I go outside, I want to see a damn bike leaning up against the damn garage."

On Christmas morning, Justin wakes up and rolls into a pile of dog poop. Confused, he walks downstairs and sees another pile under the tree. He walks outside, looks at a huge pile of dog poo by the garage, and walks inside. His dad smiles and asks, "What did Santa bring you this year?"

Justin replies, "I think I got a goddamn dog, but I can't find the son of a bitch!"

Now that's magic

A man finds a magic lamp, rubs it and a genie pops out: "I grant you three wishes, but for every wish you make, your mother-in-law gets double whatever it is you request!"

The man agrees and the genie asks for his first wish.

"I want to have £100million!" says the man. The genie duly grants his wish, but warns that his mother-in-law now has £200million.

"For my second wish," says the man, "I want to be famous!" No problem for the genie – the man is famous. But his mother-in-law is twice as famous.

Several quiet, thoughtful minutes pass before the man suggests his final wish: "Genie – beat me half to death!"

Brylcreem boy

How do you know if there's a fighter pilot at a party?
   He'll tell you.

Holy See

One day the Pope decides he's had enough of the 'No sex' rule, so he decides to treat himself to a bit of five-on-one in his bedroom. Half-way through, a window cleaner appears at his window and demands £5,000 to keep schtum, so the Pope pays him. A week later a cardinal comes round and notices how clean the windows are.

"How much did your window cleaner charge?" he asks.

"£5,000," the Pope replies.

"Christ, he must have seen you coming!"

Just got worse

There's this little man sitting in a pub, just staring into his beer. He stays like that for half an hour. Then this skinhead comes in the pub goes straight up to the guy, steals his drink and downs it in one. The little man starts crying.

Taken aback and feeling a bit guilty, the skinhead comes over all concerned. "Come on, fella," he says. "It's not that bad, is it?"

The man looks up at him and says, "Today is the worst day of my life. First, I overslept and was late to an important meeting at work. My boss fired me. When I was escorted from the building on the way to my car, I realised it had been stolen. I got a cab home and because I was early I caught my wife in bed with my best friend. I left home and came down the pub. And then, just as I was about to end it all, you show up and drink my f*cking arsenic!"

Never too old

Bert, 92, and Agnes, 89, are about to get married. They go for a stroll to discuss the wedding, and on the way they pass a chemist. Bert suggests they go in.

Bert first asks the pharmacist, "Do you sell heart medication?"

Pharmacist: "Of course."

Bert: "How about medicine for circulation?"

Pharmacist: "All kinds."

Bert: "How about Viagra?"

Pharmacist: "Of course."

Bert: "Do you sell wheelchairs and walkers?"

Pharmacist: "We do – all speeds and sizes."

Bert: "That's brilliant! We'd like to use this shop for our wedding list, please."

Well, he asked for it

Alan Shearer goes into the local supermarket and sees an old lady struggling with heavy shopping bags.

"Can you manage?" asks the boss of Newcastle United.

"No chance!" she replies angrily. "You got yourself into this mess; you can get yourself out of it!"

Sleeping partner

A man gets taken on as a lorry driver at a new company but as he's about to sign his contract in the boss's office, he says, "I've got one demand. Since you employed me, you've got to hire my mate, Dave, too."

"Who's Dave?" says the boss, surprised at the demand. "Dave's my driving partner. We're a team. He drives when I sleep, and I drive when he sleeps," the new employee says. "OK," says the boss. "Answer this question satisfactorily and I'll hire your mate too. You're going down a hill, your brakes fail, and ahead of you is a bridge with an 18-wheeler jackknifed across it. What would you do?"

"I'd wake Dave up," he replies. "How the hell's that going to help?" says the boss.

"We've been working together 25 years," explains the new guy, "and he's never seen a wreck like the one we're about to have!"

The lady is a tramp

A lady is walking down the street when a particularly shabby-looking homeless woman asks her for a couple of quid. The woman takes out a fiver, and asks, "If I give you this money, will you buy some wine with it instead of dinner?"

"No; I had to stop drinking years ago," the homeless woman replies.

"Will you use it to go shopping instead of buying food?" the woman questions again.

"No, I don't waste time shopping," the homeless woman replies. "I need to spend all my time trying to stay alive."

"Will you spend this on a beauty salon instead of food?" the woman asks.

"Are you nuts?" replies the homeless woman. "I haven't had my hair done in 20 years!"

"Well," says the woman, "I'm not going to give you the money. Instead, I'm going to take you out for dinner with my husband and myself tonight."

The homeless woman is astounded. "Won't your husband be furious with you for doing that? I know I'm dirty, and I probably smell pretty disgusting."

The woman replies, "That's OK. It's important for him to see what a woman looks like after she's given up shopping, hair appointments and wine."

Cabin pressure

A man is on a low-budget flight to Amsterdam, waiting for take-off. Another bloke comes up and says, "Excuse me, but you're in my seat."

"Don't think so. First come, first served with this airline, mate," responds the man, remaining seated.

"Look here," the newcomer insists, "I fly to Amsterdam every day and I sit in that seat every day! Now, do I have to go and get a flight attendant?"

"Get whoever you want," shrugs the seated man. Annoyed, the other man disappears for a short while and returns with a flight attendant. "I'm sorry, sir, but I'm going to have to ask you to choose another seat," she says. The man stands up, picks up his bag in a huff and says, "Fine. I didn't want to fly the plane anyway!"

Happy release

Brenda is at home making dinner, when her husband's work mate Bill arrives at her door.

"Brenda, can I come in?" he asks. "I've something to tell you."

"Of course you can come in. But where's my husband?" enquires Brenda.

"That's what I'm here to tell you, Brenda. There was an accident down at the Guinness brewery."

"Oh, God, no!" cries Brenda. "Please don't tell me."

"I must, Brenda. Your husband is dead and gone. I'm sorry."

Finally, she looks up at Bill. "How did it happen?"

"It was terrible, Brenda. He fell into a vat of Guinness and drowned."

"Oh, my dear Jesus! Did he at least go quickly?" sobbed Brenda.

"Well, no, Brenda. Fact is, he got out three times to pee."

Unkindest cut of all

A little old lady walks down the street, dragging two plastic rubbish bags with her, one in each hand. There's a hole in one of the bags, and every once in a while a £20 note flies out of it on to the pavement.

Noticing this, a policeman stops her.

"Ma'am, there are £20 notes falling out of that bag."

"Damn!" says the little old lady. "I'd better go back and see if I can still find some. Thanks for the warning!"

"Well, now, not so fast," says the cop. "How did you get all that money? Did you steal it?"

"Oh, no", says the little old lady. "You see, my back yard backs up to the car park of the football stadium and each time there's a game, a lot of fans come and pee in the bushes, right into my flowerbeds! So I go and stand behind the bushes with a big hedge clipper, and each time someone sticks his little thingie through the bushes, I say: '£20 or off it comes!'"

"Hey: not a bad idea!" laughs the cop. "By the way, what's in the other bag?"

"Well," says the little old lady, "not all of them pay."

Shellshocked

A man walks into a pub holding a turtle. The turtle has two bandaged legs, a black eye and his shell is held together with duct tape. The landlord asks, "What's wrong with your turtle?" "Nothing," the man responds. "This turtle's very fast. Have your dog stand at the end of the bar. Then go and stand at the other end of the room and call him. Before that mutt reaches you, my turtle will be there." So the landlord, wanting to see this, sets his dog at one side of the room. Then he goes to the other side and calls him. Suddenly, the guy picks up his bandaged turtle and throws it across the room, narrowly missing the landlord and smashing it into the wall. "Told you!"

Cheep at the price

A guy walks into a pet shop wanting to buy a parrot. The owner shows him a parrot that has beautiful feathers, speaks English and costs £1,000. He shows him another one with even more beautiful feathers that speaks English, French and Italian, and it can use a word processor. It costs £3,000. Then the guy sees a parrot in a cage in a corner of the shop. It's rather small and has only grey feathers. "How much for this one?"

"£5,000," replies the owner.

"£5,000!" the guy exclaims. "Does it speak foreign languages?"

"No."

"Does it have any skills?"

"Not that I know of," the owner says. "It just sits there all day."

"Then why is it £5,000?"

"The other two call it Boss."

Healing touch

Two women were playing golf. One teed off and watched in horror as her ball sailed towards a foursome of men playing the next hole. The ball hit one of the men, and he immediately clasped his groin, fell to the ground and rolled around in agony. The woman rushed down to the man and immediately began to apologise "Please let me help. I'm a physical therapist and I know I could relieve your pain if you'd allow me," she told him. "Oh, no. I'll be all right. I'll be fine in a few minutes," the man replied, still in pain.

But she persisted, and he finally allowed her to help. She gently took his hands away, loosened his trousers and put her hands inside. She began to massage him. She then asked, "How does that feel?" He replied, "It feels great, but my thumb still hurts like hell."

Man's best friend

In the middle of the night, a man phones the local vet to tell him his dog has swallowed a condom.

"You've got to help me," cries the man. "I don't know what to do."

"It's rather late," says the vet, "but, as it's an emergency, I'll be there as soon as I can."

"Hurry, please," says the owner.

"What should I do in the meantime?"

"Just keep the dog as still as you can," says the vet. "I'll get there as soon as possible."

After an hour, the vet is still driving when his mobile rings.

"I phoned earlier," says the caller. "My dog swallowed a condom."

"Yes, I know," replies the vet. "I'm going as fast as I can, but I'm stuck in traffic."

"You needn't bother," says the dog owner.

"Oh, no! Has the animal died?" cries the vet.

"No; we've found another condom in the drawer."

Keep one handy

What are woks for?
Throwing at wabbits.

Why did the leprechaun wear two condoms?
Ahh, to be sure, to be sure.

Bum's gone to Iceland

What do Eskimos get from sitting on the ice too long?
Polaroids.

My compliments to the chef

A resident in a posh hotel breakfast room calls over the head waiter one morning.

"Good morning, sir," says the waiter. "What would you like for breakfast today?"

"I'd like two boiled eggs, one of them so undercooked it's runny and the other so overcooked it's tough and hard to eat. Also, grilled bacon that has been left out so it gets a bit on the cold side; burnt toast that crumbles away as soon as you touch it with a knife; butter straight from the deep freeze so that it's impossible to spread and a pot of very weak coffee, lukewarm."

"That's a complicated order, sir," said the bewildered waiter.

"It might be quite difficult."

The guest replied, "Oh? I don't understand why. That's exactly what I got yesterday."

Cruel and unusual

What's the worst thing about Upton Park?
   The seats face the pitch.

Grab a bag today

What's Wayne Rooney's new line of pub snacks?
   Carvalho's Crushed Nuts.

That's what – ugh – you think

An old man goes to the doctor and says, "Doctor, I have this problem with farting, but it really doesn't bother me too much. They never smell and are always silent. As a matter of fact, I've farted at least 20 times since I've been here in your office. You didn't know I was passing gas, you see, because, as I say, they're odourless and noiseless." The doctor says, "I see. Take these pills and come back to see me next week."

The next week the man goes back. "Doctor," he says, "I don't know what the heck you gave me, but now when I fart they're still silent but they stink terribly."

"Good," the doctor said. "Now that we've cleared up your sinuses, let's get to work on your hearing."

Life in the Bush

What's the Aussie for foreplay?
   Brace yourself, Sheila!

Sober judgement

A man goes into a lawyer's office and says, "I heard people have sued tobacco companies for giving them lung cancer."

The lawyer says, "Yes, that's perfectly true."

The man says, "Well, I'm interested in sueing someone, too."

The lawyer says, "OK. Who are you talking about?"

The man replies, "I'd like to sue all the breweries for the ugly women I've slept with."

What's the difference between roast beef and pea soup?
Anyone can roast beef.

Dumb luck

What's the similarity between students and sperm?

Only one in a million turns out useful.

Another for the feminists

Scientists have recently suggested that men should take a look at their beer consumption, considering the results of a recent analysis that revealed the presence of female hormones in beer. The theory is that drinking beer makes men turn into women. To test the finding, 100 men were fed six pints of lager each. It was then observed that 100 per cent of the men gained weight, talked excessively without making sense, became overly emotional, couldn't drive, failed to think rationally, argued over nothing and refused to apologise when wrong. No further testing is planned.

In days of old

A brave knight has to go off to fight in the Crusades and leaves his sexy wife at home. As she can't be left alone, he fits her with a very lethal chastity belt made out of razor blades. On his victorious return, he lines up all his male staff, and makes them drop their trousers. He is greeted by a whole line of shredded todgers, apart from one. He goes up to the man and says,

"I trusted you: and, unlike all the others, you have not betrayed my trust. In return, I shall give you half my land."

To which the faithful servant replies, "Ugg ou gery muk."

Don't speak too soon

A fireman climbs up to the bedroom window of a burning house and finds a gorgeous blonde in a see-through nightie. "Aha! You're the second pregnant girl I've rescued this year," he says. "I'm not pregnant!" the blonde exclaims. "You're not rescued yet, either."

Frying tonight

A man goes into a fish 'n' chip shop with a salmon under his arm.

He asks "Do you sell fish cakes here?"

"No," comes the reply.

"Shame; it's his birthday."

His secret shame

Little David was in his primary class when the teacher asked the children what their fathers did for a living. All the typical answers came up: fireman; policeman; salesman. David was being uncharacteristically quiet, so the teacher asked him about his father. "My father's an exotic dancer in a gay cabaret and he takes off all his clothes in front of other men," he replied. The teacher, obviously shaken by this statement, took little David aside to ask him, "Is that really true about your father?"

"No," said David. "He plays for Glasgow Rangers, but I was too embarrassed to say that in front of the other kids."

Proof of life

Osama bin Laden has appeared on Al Jazeera this morning to quell rumours of his death. To prove that his appearance was not pre-recorded, Osama stated that he "watched the football and England were rubbish."

Government officials have dismissed the report, saying it could have happened any time over the last ten years.

> **Why was the Energizer Bunny arrested?**
> **He was charged with battery.**

Delicate instrument

While out on an expedition, a man is climbing over a fallen tree when his shotgun goes off, hitting him straight in the groin. Rushed to hospital, he awakes from his anaesthetic to find the surgeon has done a marvellous job repairing his damaged member. As he dresses to go home, the surgeon wanders over and hands him a business card.

"This is my brother's card. I'll make an appointment for you to see him."

The guy is shocked. "But it says here that he's a professional flute player. How can he help me?'

The doctor smiles. "Well," he says, "he's going to show you where to put your fingers so that you don't p*ss in your eye."

Trunk and disorderly

A baby boy is born with no arms, no legs and no body but his father still loves him. Eighteen years pass and the father takes his son to the pub for his first pint. The son takes his first sip and immediately he grows a torso, so the father tells him to drink again. The son takes another sip and grows some arms and legs. He's so happy he goes running into the street shouting and waving his arms around when he's suddenly hit by a lorry.

The barman shakes his head sadly. "He should have quit while he was ahead."

Insert cockatoo pun here

A honeymooning couple buy a talking parrot and take it to their room, but the groom becomes annoyed when it keeps a running commentary on his lovemaking. Finally, he throws a towel over the cage and threatens to give the bird to the zoo if it doesn't keep quiet.

Early the next morning, the couple have trouble closing a suitcase. "You get on top and I'll try," the groom instructs. But that doesn't work. The new bride figures they need more weight on top of the suitcase to shut it.

"You try getting on top," she says. Still no success. Finally, the groom says, "Look, let's both get on top."

At this point the parrot uses his beak to pull the towel off and says, "Zoo or no zoo, I have to see this!"

Dumbo and dumber

A man goes to his doctor and asks if there's a way to make his undersized penis any bigger. The doctor says there is a revolutionary surgery where a baby elephant trunk is grafted on to the end of his member. At just £3,000 for the operation the man agrees and six weeks later he's ready to try out his newly enlarged member.

While he is having dinner with his new date he feels an unusual stirring in his trousers and thinks tonight could be the night. They continue chatting over dinner when suddenly his penis flies out of his zipper, steals a bun from the table and disappears insides his trousers once more.

"Wow! Can you do that again?" asks his date, clearly impressed.

"My dick can," the man replies, "but I don't think my arse can take another bread roll."

His feminine side

Dave is at work when he notices that his colleague, Joe, is wearing an earring. Dave has always known Joe to be quite a conservative fella and is curious about his sudden change.

"Hey," he yells out. "I didn't know you were into earrings."

"Don't make such a big deal out of it," says Joe.

"No, really," probes Dave. "How long have you been wearing one?"

"Pretty much ever since my wife found it in our bed."

Smart move

Amazingly, a 65-year-old woman has a baby. All her relatives come to visit and meet the newest member of their family. They all

ask if they can see the baby, but the mother keeps saying, "Not yet."

Finally, a cousin asks, "When can we see the baby?"

"When it cries," says the elderly mother.

"But why do we have to wait until the baby cries?" the cousin asks, impatiently.

"Because I've forgotten where I've put it."

Thanks, love

What's a bloke's idea of doing housework?

Lifting his leg so you can hoover.

Birds and the bees

Little Johnny keeps asking his Dad for a television in his bedroom, to which his Dad keeps saying 'No', but after prolonged nagging, the dad agrees.

Several nights later Johnny comes downstairs and asks, "Dad, what's Love Juice?" Dad is horrified, and after looking at Mum, who's also gobsmacked, proceeds to give his son the dreaded sex talk.

Johnny now sits on sofa with his mouth open in amazement.

Dad asks, "So, what is it you've been watching then, son?"

Johnny replies, "Wimbledon."

I didn't want this job anyway

A young businessman is leaving the office late one night when he finds his boss standing over the shredder with a piece of paper in his hand.

"This is a very sensitive official document," says the boss. "My secretary's gone for the night. Can you make this thing work?"

"Sure," says the keen underling as he takes the paper, puts it in the shredder and hits the start button.

"Great," says his boss. "I just need the one copy, thanks."

Did you hear about the new French tank?

It has 14 gears. Thirteen go in reverse and one forward, in case the enemy attacks from behind.

Ask an expert

A scientific study has found that the kind of male face a woman finds attractive can differ depending on where she is in her menstrual cycle. For instance, if she is ovulating, she is attracted to men with rugged and masculine features. If she is menstruating, she is likely to prefer a man doused in petrol and set on fire, with scissors shoved deep into his temple. Further studies are expected.

Love for sale

Tom, an 80-year-old farmer, is at the doctor's telling him how he's going to marry a mail-order bride.

"How old is the new bride to be?" asks the Doc.

"She'll be twenty-one in November." Tom proudly proclaims.

Being the wise man that he is, the doctor realises that the sexual appetite of a young woman won't be satisfied by an 80-year-old man, and wanting his old patient's remaining years to be happy the doctor tactfully suggests that Tom should consider getting a hired hand to help him out on the farm, knowing nature will take its own course.

About four months later, the doctor runs into Tom on the street.

"How's the new wife?" asks the doctor.

Tom proudly says, "She's pregnant."

The doctor, happy that his sage advice has worked out, continues, "And how's the hired hand?"

Without hesitating, Tom replies, "She's pregnant too!"

Mucky business

Three dustmen are doing their last round before Christmas. The first goes to a house, knocks and finds himself being invited in by a stunning blonde, who takes him upstairs and gives him a good seeing-to.

Afterwards, he rushes out and brags to his two pals about it, so the second decides to try his luck. Sure enough, the same thing happens to him.

Finally, the dustcart driver, reckoning he's on to a sure thing, gets out and knocks on the door. The woman answers, smiles and gives him a fiver.

Severely disappointed, the man asks: 'How come I just get money, when you gave my pals a proper Christmas bonus?'

"Well," the woman replies, "when I asked my husband about tipping you all, he said 'Give the driver £5 and screw the other two.'"

Unless it was a putter, obviously

A golf club walks into a local bar and asks the barman for a pint of beer.

"Sorry, mate, but I'm not supposed to serve you," says the barman.

"Why not?" says the golf club.

"You'll be driving later," replies the bartender.

Disaster management

Bill Gates dies and goes to Heaven. At the door, Saint Peter fits him with a £5,000 suit for everything he's achieved on earth. Later, as Bill's walking around Heaven, he sees a man with a much more expensive-looking suit than his. The computer genius is extremely angry with this so he goes to Saint Peter and says, "This man has a more expensive suit than me. Who is he?"

Saint Peter says, "Ah, that's the captain of the Titanic."

Bill is furious at this and argues, "But I created the Windows operating system and I get less than him?"

Saint Peter replies, "The Titanic only crashed once!"

> **What did the redneck say to his girlfriend after breaking up with her?**
> **"Can we still be cousins?"**

You're a lifesaver

A man goes on holiday to the Caribbean, quickly falls asleep on the sand and ends up with a terrible sunburn. Wincing in pain as even a slight wind touches his scorched skin, the man hobbles off to the local doctor for help. The doctor takes one look at the man's legs and says, "I don't have anything to treat sunburn that bad. Try taking these Viagra pills."

"I've got sunburn!" cries the man. "What the hell's Viagra going to do?"

"Well, nothing for the sunburn," the doctor replies. "But it will help keep the sheets off your legs tonight."

Any port in a storm

An Aussie lass goes to her gynaecologist and tells the doctor that no matter how hard she and her husband have tried, she just can't get pregnant.

The doctor says, "OK; take off your clothes and lay down on the table."

The girl sighs and says, "Fair dos, mate: but I was really hoping to have my husband's baby."

His and hearse

A man was passing through a small town when he came upon a huge funeral procession.

"Who died?" he asked a nearby local.

"I'm not sure," replied the local, "but I think it's the one in the coffin."

The little woman

A man is giving a colleague a lift to work and asks him if he talks to his wife after sex.

"Absolutely," he says. "If I can find a phone."

Land of the brave, home of the free

A redneck is walking down the road and sees his cousin coming toward him with a sack.

"What you got there?" he asks.

"Some chickens," replies his equally slack-jawed cousin.

"If I can guess how many you got, can I have one?"

"Shoot. If you guess right, I'll give you both of 'em."

"OK... five."

Keeping it in the family

What do you call the sweat that's produced when a Norfolk couple have sex?

Relative humidity.

I'm afraid our time is up...

A woman went to her psychiatrist because she was having problems with her sex life. The psychiatrist asked her many questions. Finally, he asked, "Do you ever watch your husband's face while you're having sex?"

"Well, yes, I actually did once," replied the woman.

"And tell me, how did your husband look?" asked the psychiatrist.

"Angry. Fuming, actually," replied the woman.

At this point, the psychiatrist felt that he was getting somewhere and said, "Well, that's interesting. How did it occur that you saw his face that time?"

"He was looking at me through the window!"

Hi, Ena

Wife to husband: "Who was that lady I seen you with last night?"

Husband: "You mean 'I saw.'"

Wife: "OK; who was that eyesore I seen you with last night?"

175

Oldest trick in the book

A minister is winding up his sermon one Sunday in church.

"Next Sunday I am going to preach on the subject of liars: and in this connection, as a preparation for my discourse, I would like you all to read the seventeenth chapter of Mark," he says.

On the following Sunday, the vicar walks to the front of the church and says, "Now, then, all of you who have done as I requested and read the seventeenth chapter of Mark, please raise your hands."

Nearly every hand in the congregation shoots up.

The vicar looks stern and says, "You are the ones I want to talk to about lying. There is no seventeenth chapter of Mark."

A man walks into a record shop and asks, "What have you got by The Doors?"
The owner replies, "A mop and a fire extinguisher."

Snap diagnosis

While making his rounds, a doctor points out an X-ray to a group of medical students.

"As you can see," he begins, "the patient has a limp because his left fibula and tibia are radically arched."

The doctor turns to one of the students and asks, "What would you do in a case like this?"

"Well," ponders the student, "I suppose I'd limp, too."

Works like a charm

A man approaches a beautiful woman in a supermarket and asks, "You know, I've lost my wife here in the supermarket. Can you talk to me for a couple of minutes?"

"Why?" she asks.

"Because every time I talk to a beautiful woman, my wife appears out of nowhere."

Can you keep it down?

An Aussie walks into a library and asks the librarian, "Excuse me, mate, can I have a burger and large fries, please?"

Tutting, the bookworm replies: "Excuse me, sir; this is a library."

The Aussie leans over the counter. "I'm sorry, mate," he whispers. "Can I have a burger and large fries, please?"

Notional Elf Service

A man walks into the doctor and says, "I have a recurring dream in which I'm writing *Lord of the Rings*. It's really disturbing"

The doctor says, "I'm afraid you're Tolkien in your sleep."

Too close

A guy goes into a girl's house and she shows him into the living room. She excuses herself to go to the kitchen to make some drinks. As he's standing there alone, he notices a vase on the mantelpiece. He picks it up and as he's looking at it, she walks back in. He says, "What's this?"

"Oh, my father's ashes are in there," she replies. Turning red, he apologizes.

She continues, "Yeah, he's too lazy to go to get an ashtray."

Clinical finishing

Saddam Hussein is found guilty at his trial and is asked by the judge if he has any final wishes.

"I want to choose my firing squad," demands the dictator.

"I guess that would be OK," replied the judge.

"Great," says Saddam. "I want Lampard, Gerrard and Carragher from 12 yards."

Is this it?

Not long after their wedding, Scott and Lisa awake early one morning. They are up for quite a while before they meet in the kitchen. Marriage has been agreeing with Scott, and he greets his new wife with glee.

"Sweetheart," he says, "if you'll just make the toast and pour the juice, breakfast will be ready."

"Great! What are we having?" asks Lisa.

"Toast and juice," replies Scott.

> **Did you hear about the guy in hospital for sniffing curry powder?**
> **He's in a korma.**

Wonderful for her age

Three sisters aged 92, 94 and 96 live in a house together. One night the 96-year-old runs a bath. She puts her foot in and pauses. She yells to the other sisters, "Was I getting in or out of the bath?"

The 94-year-old yells back, "I don't know. I'll come up and see."

She starts up the stairs and pauses, "Was I going up the stairs or down?" she shouts.

The 92-year-old is sitting at the kitchen table having tea listening to her sisters. She shakes her head and says, "I sure hope I never get that forgetful... knock on wood."

She then yells, "I'll come up and help both of you as soon as I see who's at the door."

Do you have it in pink?

A woman walks into a gun shop and asks the salesman if he can help her pick out a rifle. "It's for my husband," she explains.

"Did he tell you what calibre to get?" asks the salesman.

"Are you kidding? He doesn't even know I'm going to shoot him."

Survival of the fittest

Two campers are walking through the woods when a huge brown bear suddenly appears in the clearing about 50 feet in front of them. The bear sees the campers and begins to head toward them. The first guys drops his backpack, digs out a pair of trainers and frantically begins to put them on.

The second guy says: "What are you doing? Trainers won't help you outrun that bear."

"I don't need to outrun the bear," the first bloke says. "I just need to outrun you."

Poultry in motion

Why does a chicken coop have two doors?

If it had four, it would be a chicken sedan.

Grounds for divorce?

An old woman visits her doctor to ask his help in reviving her husband's libido.

"What about trying Viagra?" asks the doctor.

"Not a chance", she says. "He won't even take an aspirin."

"Not a problem", replies the doctor. "Drop it into his coffee. He won't even taste it. Give it a try and call me in a week to let me know how things went."

It wasn't a week later that she ends up calling the doctor.

"It was horrid: just terrible, doctor," cries the old dear.

"Really? What happened?" asks the doctor.

"Well, I did as you advised and slipped it in his coffee and the effect was almost immediate! He jumped straight up, with a twinkle in his eye, and ripped my clothes to tatters and took me then and there."

"Why so terrible?" asks the doctor, "Was the sex that bad?"

"Oh, no, doctor," says the old lady. "It was the best sex I've had in 25 years! But I'll never be able to show my face in Starbucks again."

> **Did you hear about the man who fell into the machine at the upholsterer's factory?**
> **He's fully recovered.**

He's got you there

A mechanic was removing the cylinder head from the engine of a Jaguar when he spotted a well-known heart surgeon in his garage, who was waiting for the service manager to look at his car. The mechanic shouted across the garage, "Hey, Doc. Could I ask you a question?"

The surgeon, a bit surprised, walked over to the mechanic. The mechanic straightened up, wiped his hands on a rag and asked, "So, Doc, take a look at this engine. I open its heart, take valves out, fix 'em, put 'em back in, and when I finish, it works just like new. So how come I get such a small salary and you get loads of money when you and I are doing basically the same work?"

The surgeon paused, smiled and leaned over, and then whispered to the mechanic, "Try doing it with the engine running."

The customer is always right

A man walks into a bank and says to the clerk, "I want to open a bloody account, you total, utter moron!"

"I'm sorry, sir?" says the clerk, taken aback.

"I said I want to open a bloody account, you dim-witted fool."

Offended by the attitude of the man, the clerk warns the customer that he doesn't have to put up with this sort of abuse and promptly leaves. Returning with the manager, he explains the situation.

"Well, sir, it seems we have a problem," says the manager.

"You're right," says the man. "I've won 50 million quid and want to open an account with you."

"I see," says the manager looking at his clerk, "so it's this idiot here that's the problem then."

What did the Mexican fireman name his twins?
Hose A and Hose B.

Prune in autumn

Two old men are sitting outside the town hall, where a flower show is in progress. One complains, "Cripes, life is boring. We never have any fun! For £10, I'll streak naked through the flower show!"

"You're on!" the other geriatric shouts.

The first old man fumbles out of his clothes and streaks through the hall. Waiting outside, his friend hears a commotion, followed by applause. Then the naked old man bursts through the door, surrounded by a cheering crowd. "How did it go?" asks the friend.

"Great!" says the wrinkled streaker. "I won first prize for dried arrangement!"

Good book

A priest who has to spend the night in a hotel asks the girl in reception to come up to his room for dinner.

After a while he makes a pass at her, but she stops him and reminds him that he is a holy man.

"It's OK," he replies, "it's written in the Bible."

After a wild night of sex she asks to see where in the Bible it says it's OK.

The priest rolls over, takes the Gideon bible out of the desk by the bed and shows her the first page. On it, someone has scrawled: "The girl in reception will shag anyone."

They think of everything

Why are there so many tree-lined boulevards in France?

Germans like to march in the shade.

We come in peace for all mankind

A NASA crew destined for a moon landing was training near a Navajo Indian reservation. A Navajo elder asked if he could send a message to the moon with the astronauts. The NASA crew agreed, then called in a translator. The message said, "Watch out for these guys. They have come to steal your land."

Fitting right in

A bright young Scottish lad named Gordie has the opportunity to go to university in London, so he packs his bags and says goodbye to his mother and leaves the highlands for the big city. After the first week his mother calls to see how her boy is holding up.

"I love it here Mother," Gordie tells her, "but these English students are the oddest people ever! Why, the boy who lives in the dormitory room next to me bangs his head against the wall until midnight every night. And the boy in the room above me stomps around until midnight every night. And the boy right below me blasts his stereo until midnight every night."

"Why don't you complain to the Dean of Students?" asks his mother.

"Well, it doesn't bother me much," answers Gordie. "I'm usually up until that time practicing my bagpipes anyway."

Playing around

One day, a man came home early from work and was greeted by his wife dressed in very sexy lingerie and high heels. "Tie me up," she purred, "and you can do anything you want." So he tied her up and went golfing.

Filled with the holy spirit

Jade Goody is looking in a mirror and her fluctuating weight is depressing her. In an act of desperation, she decides to call on God for help. "God if you take away my love handles, I'll devote my life to you," she prays. And just like that, her ears fall off.

Investor in people

An office manager arrives at his department and sees an employee sitting behind his desk, totally stressed out. He gives him a spot of advice: "I went home every afternoon for two weeks and had myself pampered by my wife. It was fantastic, and it really helped me. Maybe you should give it a try, too."

Two weeks later, when the manager arrives at his department, he sees the same man happy and full of energy at his desk. The faxes are piling up, and the computer is running at full speed.

"Excellent," says the manager, "I see you followed my advice."

"I did," answers the employee. "It was great! By the way, I didn't know you had such a nice house!"

What goes, "Click. Is that it? Click. Is that it? Click. Is that it?"?
A blindfolded man doing a Rubik's Cube.

Gee, thanks

A woman rushes downstairs into the foyer of a large hotel and screams at the receptionist, "Check me out! I'm in a hurry!"

The receptionist eyes her up for a second and says, "Not bad, but your bum's a bit big."

Extreme lengths

An extremely drunk man looking for a brothel stumbles blindly into a chiropodist's office instead. He weaves over to the receptionist. Without looking up, she waves him over to the examination bed.

"Stick it through that curtain," she says. Looking forward to something kinky, the drunk whips out his penis and sticks it through the crack in the curtains.

"That's not a foot!" screams the receptionist.

"Christ!" replies the drunk. "I didn't know you had a minimum."

You got me there

One night, a policewoman pulls over a drunk driver. She asks him to step out of his car and says, "Anything you say can and will be held against you." The drunk thinks about this for a moment and says, "Breasts."

Spend, spend, spend

What do men and money in the bank have in common?

Both lose interest after withdrawal.

If only they could talk

Little Johnny is sitting in a biology class, and the teacher says that an interesting phenomenon of nature is that only humans stutter; no other animal in the world does this. Johnny's hand shoots up.

"Not correct, Miss!" he says.

"Please explain, Johnny," replies the teacher.

"Well, Miss, the other day I was playing with my cat. The neighbours' pitbull came around the corner, and my cat went 'fffffffff! fffffffffff! fffffffff!', and before he could say 'f*ck off!', the dog ate him!"

Living dangerously

A man walks into a pub with a neck brace, orders a pint and asks the landlord, "Who's in the lounge?"

The landlord replies, "There's 15 people playing darts."

The man says, "Get them a pint, too." Then he asks, "Who's upstairs?"

The landlord replies, "150 people at the disco."

The man says, "Get them pints too."

"That'll be £328, please," says the landlord.

The man replies, "Sorry, I haven't got that much money on me."

The landlord remarks, "If you were at the pub down the road, they'd have broken your neck."

"Just been there," says the man.

And make it snippy

A man visits his GP with a delicate matter: "I was thinking about getting a vasectomy."

"Well, that's a big decision," says the doctor. "Have you talked it over with your family?"

"Oh, yes," says the man. "They're in favour of it, 15 to seven."

What do a farmer and a pimp have in common?
Both need a hoe to stay in business.

It's Miller time

After striking gold in Alaska, a lonely miner walks down from the mountains and into a saloon in the nearest town.

"I'm lookin' for the meanest, toughest, roughest hooker you got," he says to the barman.

"We got her," he replies. "She's upstairs in the second room on the right."

The miner hands the pint-puller a gold nugget to pay for the lady of the night and two beers. He grabs the bottles, stomps up the stairs, kicks open the door and yells, "I'm looking for the meanest, roughest, toughest hooker in town."

The woman inside the room looks at the miner and says, "You found her!" Then she strips naked, bends over and grabs her ankles.

"How do you know I want to do you like that?" asks the miner.

"I don't," replies the hooker, "I just thought you might like to open those beers first."

All mod cons

Proudly showing off his new apartment to some friends late one night, a drunk leads the way to his bedroom. When they get there, they see that there's a big brass gong taking pride of place.

"What's with that gong?" one of the friends asks.

"That's no gong," the drunk replies. "It's a talking clock!"

"Oh yeah? How does it work, then?" the friend asks.

"Watch," the drunk says. He moves to the corner of the room, picks up a hammer and pounds the gong as loudly as he can. Suddenly, someone on the other side of the wall starts screaming, "What the hell do you think you're doing? It's three o'clock in the bloody morning!"

Battle beyond the stars

Luke Skywalker goes to his lightsaber practice with Yoda carrying a spoon.

"What curious object is that?" asks Yoda.

"It's the spoon that I've used since I was a little boy," replies Luke. "I take it everywhere I go and keep it in my shirt pocket at all times."

Unimpressed, Yoda puts Luke through his paces with an intense lightsaber battle and in the heat of the duel Yoda delivers a stinging blow to Luke's chest, but the little green fella's lightsaber strikes Luke's spoon. It shatters, saving the Jedi's life.

That night at dinner in Yoda's hut, Luke is thinking about the loss of his spoon, his most prized possession after his lightsaber.

"Moping stop you," demands Yoda. "My wooden spoon use you; just as good it is."

But Yoda's new spoon just doesn't feel right.

"I'll never be able to eat again!" cries the young Jedi.

Suddenly, Obi-wan appears hovering above his plate.

"Luke," says the Jedi Master. "Use the fork."

It never fails

A man walks into a pub and immediately spots a gorgeous woman standing at the bar. The man strides up to her and, by way of a chat-up line, says, "Do you want to see some magic?"

"What sort of magic?" the intrigued lady asks.

"You come back home with me, have sex and then disappear."

Now we are six

A little girl walks in to the lounge one Sunday morning where her Dad is reading the paper.

"Where does poo come from?" she asks.

Father, feeling a little perturbed that his five-year-old daughter is already asking difficult questions, thinks for a moment and says:

"Well, you know we just ate breakfast?"

"Yes," replies the girl.

"Well, the food goes into our tummies and our bodies take out all the good stuff, and then whatever's left over comes out of our bottoms when we go to the toilet. That's poo."

The little girl looks perplexed, and stares at him in stunned silence for a few seconds and asks: "And Tigger?"

Life lesson

A little girl returns home from school and announces that a friend has told her where babies come from. Amused, her mother replies, "Why don't you tell me all about it?" The little girl explains, "Well, mummy and daddy take off all their clothes, and then daddy's thingy stands up, and then the mummy puts it in her mouth, and then it sort of explodes." Her mother shakes her head, leans over to meet her eye-to-eye, and says, "Oh, that's sweet, but that's not how you get babies. That's how you get jewellery."

> **What's the last thing a drummer says before leaving a band?**
> **"Why don't we try one of my songs?"**

Let's call it quits

A man who hates his wife's cat decides to get rid of it by driving it to the next town and leaving it there. But when he gets home, the cat's already back. The next day, he drops the cat off even further away, but the same thing happens. Finally, the man dumps the cat hundreds of miles away. Hours later, the man calls home to his wife: "Honey, is the cat there?"

"Yes," she says.

"Can you put him on? I'm lost."

The finer things

A man finds a genie in a bottle, and is offered three wishes. First he asks for a fast sports car. Suddenly, a Ferrari appears before him. Next, he asks for a big house. Suddenly, he's sitting in a huge mansion. Finally, he asks to be made irresistible to women. Suddenly, he turns into a box of luxury chocolates.

Last request

Two men were asked what they would like to be said about them at their funerals. The first one said, "I want someone to say I was the greatest footballer ever." The other man said, "I want someone to say, 'He's moving, he's moving!'"

The divine plan

Three men are arguing in a pub. The first says, "God must be a mechanical engineer; just look at the joints in the human body." The second says, "God's an electrical engineer; look at the nervous system." The third says, "God has to be a civil engineer; who else would run a waste disposal pipeline through a perfectly good recreational area?"

Flying rats

The Mayor of London is worried because pigeon crap is ruining the streets and it's costing a fortune to keep them clean.

One day a man arrives at the London Assembly building and offers the Mayor a proposition: "I can rid your beautiful city of its plague of pigeons without cost to the city, but you must promise not to ask me any questions: or, you can pay me £5 million and ask one question." The Mayor considers the offer and accepts.

Next day the man climbs to the top of the London Assembly building, opens his coat and releases a blue pigeon that flies up into the sky. All the pigeons in London see it and they follow it out of the city. The next day the blue pigeon returns completely alone to the man and the Mayor is suitably impressed.

Even though the pigeon fancier-charges nothing, the Mayor presents him with a cheque for five million quid.

"You have done the city and the people of London a wonderful service," he declares, "but I have paid you five million pounds so that I can ask you one question."

"Fire away," says the man.

"By any chance, do you know where we can find a blue Australian?" the Mayor asks.

The perfect gift

Two friends are sitting at a bar shooting the breeze over a couple of jars.

"I got my wife a diamond ring for her birthday," says one guy.

"Didn't you tell me she wanted an SUV?" asks his pal.

"Yeah, but I couldn't find a fake Range Rover."

A lump in the throat

A man goes to a barbershop for a shave. While the barber is lathering him up, he mentions the problems he has getting a close shave around the cheeks.

"I have just the thing," says the barber, taking a small wooden ball from a nearby drawer. "Just place this between your cheek and gum."

The man places the ball in his mouth and the barber proceeds with the closest shave the man has ever experienced. After a few strokes, the client asks in garbled speech, "But what if I swallow it?"

"No problem," says the barber. "Just bring it back tomorrow like everyone else does."

What do you call a guy born in Leeds, who grows up in Edinburgh and dies in Liverpool?
Dead.

New man

Three Aussies were working on a high-rise building project – Steve, Bruce and Bluey. Steve falls off and is killed instantly. As the ambulance takes the body away, Bruce says, "Someone should go and tell his wife."

Bluey says, "OK. I'm pretty good at that sensitive stuff, so let me do it." Two hours later, he comes back carrying a crate of beer. Bruce says, "Where did you get that from, Bluey?"

"Steve's wife gave it to me," Bluey replies.

"That's unbelievable," says Bruce. "You told the lady her husband was dead and she gave you the beer?"

"Well, not exactly," Bluey says. "When she answered the door, I said to her, 'You must be Steve's widow.' She said, 'I'm not a widow.' And I said, 'I'll bet you a crate of beer you are'."

Intimate strangers

One day at a bus stop there's a girl wearing a skin-tight miniskirt.

Just as she's about to get on the bus she realises that her skirt is so tight she can't lift her foot high enough to reach the first step.

Thinking it will give her enough slack to raise her leg, she reaches back and unzips her skirt a little. However, she can't reach the step, so she reaches back once again to unzip it a little more, but still she can't reach the step. So, with her skirt zipper halfway down, she reaches back and unzips her skirt all the way. Thinking that she can get on the step now, she lifts up her leg, only to realize it's still impossible.

Seeing how embarrassed the girl is, the man standing behind her puts his hands around her waist and lifts her up on to the first step of the bus. The girl turns around furiously and screams, "How dare you touch me that way? I don't even know you!"

Shocked, the man says, "Well, after you reached around and unzipped my fly three times, I figured that we were friends."

Bad decision

A Ukrainian woman bumps into the Chelsea football squad in a nightclub. She approaches John Terry and asks for his autograph on her breast. Terry agrees, and she obliges by lifting up her top so that he can sign her left one. She then asks Drogba for his autograph on her other breast. Drogba willingly agrees, and she obliges by lifting up her top so he can sign the right one. She then asks Mourinho for his autograph somewhere a bit more private. Jose agrees and the woman obliges by dropping her knickers. Suddenly, Mourinho turns white and says, "On second thoughts, I think I'll pass. The last time I signed a Ukrainian twat it cost me £30 million."

A breed apart

A young entrepreneur starts his own business. He is shrewd and diligent, so business keeps coming in. Pretty soon he realises that he needs an in-house counsel, and so he begins interviewing young lawyers.

"As I'm sure you can understand," he starts off with one of the first applicants, "in a business like this, our personal integrity must be beyond question." He leans forward. "Mr. Peterson, are you an 'honest' lawyer?"

"Honest?" replies the job prospect. "Let me tell you something about honesty. I'm so honest that my dad lent me £15,000 for my education and I paid back every penny the minute I completed my very first case."

"Impressive. And what sort of case was that?"

"My father filed a small claims suit against me."

> **What do you call a lawyer with an IQ of 50?**
> **Your Honour.**

The old enemy

A family of England supporters head out one Saturday to get their new football kits. In the sports shop the son picks up a Scotland football shirt and says to his sister, "I've decided I'm going to be a Scotland supporter."

The sister is outraged at this, promptly whacks him round the head and says, "Go talk to your mother!"

The lad goes off and finds his mother. "Mum, I've decided I'm going to be a Scotland supporter and I want this shirt."

The mother is outraged and promptly whacks him round the head and says, "Go talk to your father."

Off goes the lad again and finds his father. "Dad, I've decided I'm going to be a Scotland supporter and I want this shirt."

The father is outraged, promptly whacks his son round the head and says, "No son of mine is ever going to be seen in that!"

About half an hour later, they're all back in the car heading home. The father turns to the son and says, "Son, I hope you have learned something today?"

The son turns to his dad and says, "Yes, I have."

"Good, son, what is it?" says the dad.

The son replies, "I've only been a Scotland supporter for an hour and I already hate you English bastards!"

Miracle of science

Bored over the summer, Jonathan Woodgate goes shopping, and sees something interesting in the kitchen department of a large store.

"What's that?" he asks.

"A Thermos flask," replies the assistant.

"What does it do?" asks Jonathan.

The assistant tells him it keeps hot things hot and cold things cold. Really impressed, Jonathan buys one and takes it along to his next training session with Real Madrid.

"Here, boys, look at this," he says proudly. "It's a Thermos flask."

The lads are impressed.

"What does it do?" they ask.

"It keeps hot things hot and cold things cold, "says Jonathan.

"And what have you got in it?" asks Raul.

"Two cups of coffee and a choc ice," replies Woodgate.

No wonder they made him the schoolteacher

The residents of a redneck town keep falling down a deep hole in the middle of its main street and always end up dying because the nearest hospital is located some 40 miles away. The mayor calls a town meeting to address the issue and asks for suggestions.

"We need our own hospital!" suggests one local.

"That's beyond our budget," answers the mayor. "Anyone else got any ideas?"

"I got a perfect idea," says another hick. "Just dig the hole next to the hospital."

Under the knife

Four surgeons took a coffee break and discussed their work. The first said, "I think accountants are the easiest to operate on. You open them up and everything inside is numbered." The second said, "Librarians are easier. You open them up and everything is alphabeticised." The third said, "I like to operate on electricians. You open them up and everything inside is colour-coded." The fourth one said, "I like to operate on lawyers. They're heartless, spineless, gutless and their heads and their arses are interchangeable."

Two minds with but a single thought

During a boring blind date, a man takes a call from a friend. He leaves the table to answer it and decides it gives him an opportunity to escape. When he returns to his date he looks upset and says, "I'm afraid my grandad's just died. I must go."

"I understand," says the girl. "If yours hadn't died, mine would have had to."

With friends like these

The Lone Ranger and Tonto are riding in the desert when hostile Apaches surround them. The Lone Ranger turns to his trusted sidekick and says, "It looks like we're in trouble, old friend."

Tonto replies, "Who the hell are you, paleface?"

Filth commandment

A minister was asked to dinner by one of his parishioners, whom he knew was a slovenly housekeeper. When he sat down at the table, he noticed that the dishes were the dirtiest that he had ever seen in his life.

"Were these dishes ever washed?" he asked his hostess, running his fingers over the grit and grime.

She replied, "They're as clean as soap and water could get them."

He felt a bit apprehensive, but blessed the food anyway and started eating. It was really delicious and he said so, despite the dirty dishes.

When dinner was over, the hostess took the dishes outside and yelled, to her dogs "Here, Soap! Here, Water!"

What do you get when you cross LSD with a birth control pill?
A trip without the kids.

Personal hygiene

One night, a man rolls over in bed and gives his wife a big, knowing grin. Immediately realising his intentions she says, "Not tonight darling. I have an appointment with the gynaecologist tomorrow morning and I want to stay fresh and clean."

Dejected and disappointed, the man rolls over and tries to get to sleep. A few minutes later he rolls over and prods his wife again.

"Tell me; do you have a dental appointment tomorrow, too?"

Lead, kindly light

Two men meet while walking their dogs through a graveyard. One says to the other, "Morning."

The second man replies, "No, just walking the dog."

Slow learner

One morning four golfers are waiting at the men's tee, while a foursome of ladies are hitting from the ladies' tee. The ladies take their time but finally the last woman is ready to tee off. She hacks it about 10 feet, curses, walks over to the ball and hacks it another 10 feet.

She looks up at the watching men, shrugs and says, "I guess all those f**king lessons I took this winter didn't help."

One of the guys replies, "Now there's your problem. You should've taken golf lessons instead. Still, d'ya fancy a drink?"

Comfortably numb

What's the ultimate rejection?

You're masturbating, and your hand falls asleep.

Law of the jungle

A missionary has spent years teaching agriculture and 'civilization' to some people in a distant land. One day, he wants to start teaching them English. So he takes the tribal chief and points at a tree.

"Tree," says the missionary.

"Tree," mimics the chief.

The holy man then points to a rock.

"Rock," he says.

"Rock," copies the chief.

All of a sudden, they come upon two people having sex in the bushes. Embarrassed, the missionary blurts out that they are 'riding a bike.' Then the chief pulls out his blowpipe and shoots the two people.

"What are you doing?" yells the missionary. "I've spent all this time civilizing you, and you turn around and do this!"

"My bike," says the chief.

Match of the day

How do you make Robbie Savage go woof?

Douse him in petrol and set him on fire.

We've all got to go some time

A man goes to his doctor for a complete check-up. Afterwards, the doctor comes out with the results. "I'm afraid I have some bad news," says the doctor. "You don't have much time."

"Oh, no, that's terrible. How long have I got?" the man asks.

"Ten," says the doctor.

"Ten what? Months? Weeks?"

"Nine..." continues the doctor.

Bombe surprise

What do you get when a grenade is thrown into a French kitchen?

Linoleum Blownapart.

Why was the pasty in the pub?
He was meetin' potato.

We have lift-off

Dave and Jim worked as aeroplane mechanics in London. One day, the airport was fogbound and they were stuck in the hangar. Dave said, "I wish we had a drink."

"Me, too," replied Jim. "Y'know, I've heard you can drink jet fuel and get a buzz. You want to try it?" So they poured themselves a couple of glasses and got completely smashed. The next morning, Dave woke up and was surprised at how good he felt. Then the phone rang and it was Jim.

"Hey, how do you feel this morning?" he asked.

"I feel great," said Dave. "How about you?"

"I feel great, too." Jim responded.

"Have you broken wind yet?"

"No," said Dave.

"Well, don't – I'm in Glasgow!"

Blame game

While out for a drive, an elderly couple stop at a service station for lunch. Back on the road afterwards, the elderly woman realises that she's left her glasses in the service station.

By then, they've travelled quite a distance and have to go even further before they can find a place to turn around.

The old fella moans and complains all the way back to the restaurant. He called his wife every name he can think of and when they finally arrive back at the service station, and the woman gets out of the car to retrieve her glasses, the man yells to her, "And while you're in there, you might as well get my wallet, too!"

That stuff goes right through you

A skeleton walks into a bar. The barman asks, "What can I get you?" The skeleton replies, "I'll have a pint of lager and a mop, please."

Man and superman

A big city promoter hears of a man who has 20 wives who he makes love to every day. Impressed, the promoter hires the man to exhibit his prowess on stage in London's West End. On opening night it all goes wrong, when the man makes love to only 10 of his wives before he collapses with exhaustion.

The curtain falls, and the promoter rushes up to his failed investment. "What happened?" he asks.

"I don't know," the man answers. "Everything went fine in rehearsal!"

Just a nip

A man walking down the street sees a woman with perfect breasts. He says to her, "Excuse me, miss, but would you let me bite your breasts for £100?"

"Are you mad?" she replies, and keeps walking. He turns around, runs around the block and gets to the corner before she does.

"Would you let me bite your breasts for £1,000?" he asks again.

"Listen, you, I'm not that kind of woman! Got it?" The man will not give up and catches up with her again. "OK, final offer. Would you let me bite your breasts, just once, for £10,000?"

She thinks about it for a while and says, "£10,000, eh? OK, just once."

She takes off her blouse to reveal the most perfect breasts in the world. As soon as he sees them, he grabs them and starts caressing them, fondling them slowly, kissing them and burying his face in them, but not biting them. The woman finally gets annoyed and asks, "Well? Are you going to bite them or not?"

"Nah," he replies. "Too expensive."

The first cuckold of spring

A guy comes home from work, walks into his bedroom, and finds a stranger making love to his wife. He says, "What the hell are you two doing?"

His wife turns to the stranger and says, "I told you he was stupid."

Upscale dining

A man walks into a Japanese restaurant with his wife. The waiter approaches, and the man asks for a table for two. As they are waiting for a table to be prepared, his wife notices a tank full of beautiful tropical fish.

The wife turns to her husband and says that she wants the same fish for a tank at home. The husband agrees and asks the waiter what the fish are called.

The waiter replies, "Sushi, sir."

What's grey, eats fish and lives in Washington DC?
The Presidential Seal.

Down, boy

Two men walking down the road see a dog licking its balls.

The first man says, "I wish I could do that."

The second man replies, "Better stroke him first – he might bite."

All that kneeling

A drunk man sits down on a train seat next to a priest. The man's tie is stained, his face is plastered with red lipstick and a half-empty bottle of gin is sticking out of his torn coat pocket. He opens his newspaper and begins reading.

After a few minutes the man turns to the priest and asks, "Say, Father, what causes arthritis?"

"My Son, it's caused by loose living, sleeping with wanton women, drinking too much alcohol and having contempt for your fellow-man," the priest replies.

"Well, I'll be damned," the drunk mutters, returning to his paper.

The priest, thinking about what he said, nudges the man and apologises. "I'm very sorry. I didn't mean to come on so strong. How long have you had arthritis?"

"I don't, Father," the man says. "I was just reading here that the Pope does."

God sees all

During his wedding rehearsal, the groom approached the vicar and said, "Look, I'll give you £100 if you'll change the wedding vows and miss out the 'love, honour and obey' part." He passed the clergyman the cash and left the church satisfied.

On his wedding day, when it came time for the groom's vows, the vicar looked the young man in the eye and said: "Will you promise to love, honour and obey her every command and wish, serve her breakfast in bed every morning and swear that you will never look at another woman, as long as you both shall live?" The groom gulped and said in a squeaky voice, "Yes."

He then leaned toward the vicar and hissed through clenched teeth, "I thought we had a deal?"

The vicar looked at the bride.

"She made me a better offer."

Boom-boom!

Three blokes with dogs walk into a pub. The first orders a
bottle of beer and, when it comes, his dog pours it for him. The
second orders a beer, and his dog opens some crisps. The third
orders a beer but, when it comes, his dog just sits there.

"Your dog doesn't do any tricks?" asks the first guy.

"He's a blacksmith," says the third.

"What do you mean?"

"If you pour beer over him, he'll make a bolt for the door."

Land of smiles

Where would you be without a sense of humour?

Germany.

Plastered again

Mike staggers home very late after another late night drinking
session with his best mates and removes his shoes to avoid
waking his missus. He tiptoes as quietly as he can towards the
stairs but trips and knocks a vase on to the floor, which he
then falls on to, cutting his buttocks. Managing not to shout,
he stands up and pulls his pants down to examine the damage
in the hall mirror. His backside is cut and bleeding, so he
grabs a box of plasters and sticks them wherever he can see
blood. He then hides the almost empty plaster box and
stumbles into bed.

The next morning, Mike awakes with searing pain in both his head and arse, to see his wife staring at him.

"You were drunk again last night, weren't you?" she says.

"Why would you say such a mean thing?" he asks.

"Well," she says, "it could be the open front door. Or the broken glass at the bottom of the stairs. Or the drops of blood on the stairs. It could even be your bloodshot eyes: but mostly, it's all those bloody plasters stuck to the hall mirror!"

> **What do you call a judge with no thumbs?**
> **Justice Fingers.**

Miss! Miss!

A customer wanted to ask his attractive waitress for a date but couldn't get her attention. When he was finally able to catch her eye, she quickly looked away. Finally, he followed her into the kitchen and blurted out his invitation. To his amazement, she said yes. So he asked, "Why have you been avoiding me all this time? You wouldn't even make eye contact with me."

"Oh," replied the waitress, "I just thought you were after more coffee."

Hanging up his gloves

Who was the last person to box Rocky Marciano?
  His undertaker.

Great puns of our time no. 94

Saint George went to a transvestite party and said: "How do you like me with my drag on?"

The pits

After a particularly gruelling F1 race, Flavio Briatore is sitting on his luxury yacht in Monaco harbour sipping some white wine. On the TV is a documentary about how unemployed youths from Liverpool can remove a set of wheels in less than six seconds with no proper equipment.

Flavio is amazed by this and immediately fires Renault's entire pit crew, who can only do it in eight seconds with millions of Euros-worth of high-tech equipment at their disposal. Taking advantage of one of Tony Blair's youth opportunity schemes, Flavio fills the vacant places in Renault's garage with the youths from the documentary.

At the crew's first practice the racing bigwig is amazed as the young Scousers successfully change the tyres of Giancarlo Fisichella's car in less than six seconds, and he walks away confident that Renault will take the F1 crown again this season.

Suddenly, his mobile phone rings. It's Briatore's boss, the President of Renault.

"Have you seen those new guys in the pit?" brags Briatore. "No one can stop us this year. It only took them six seconds to change the tyres."

"You idiot!" comes the reply from the company president. "Within 12 seconds they'd resprayed, rebadged and sold the car to Red Bull for eight bottles of Heineken and some photos of David Coulthard's bird in the shower!"

Glued to the box

Why do rednecks like having sex doggie-style?

So they can both watch *American Idol*.

Second opinion

A beautiful woman about to undergo a minor operation is lying on a trolley in a hospital corridor awaiting the doctors. A man in a white coat approaches, lifts up the sheet and examines her naked body. He walks away and confers with another man in a white coat. He approaches and does the same thing.

When a third man approaches her, she asks impatiently, "These examinations are fine, but when are you going to start the operation?"

He shrugs and says, "Your guess is as good as mine, lady. We're just here to paint the corridor."

How many men do you need for a Mafia funeral?
Just one. To slam the car boot shut.

Telling it straight

A teacher says to her class, "I'm going to call on each of you and you're going to tell me what your father does for a living. Tommy, you're first."

Tommy says, "My father's a doctor."

The teacher says, "Jamie, what about you?"

Jamie says, "My father's a lawyer."

Finally, there's one boy left and the teacher says, "Billy, what does your father do?"

Billy replies, "My father's dead, Miss."

Shocked, the teacher says, "I'm so sorry. What did he do before he died?"

Billy says, "He turned purple and collapsed on the dog, Miss."

Answer that!

God is sitting in Heaven when a scientist says to him, "Lord, we don't need you any more. Science has finally figured out a way to create life out of nothing. We can now do what you did in the beginning."

"Oh, is that so? Tell me," replies God.

"Well," says the scientist, "we can take dirt and breathe life into it, thus creating man."

"Well, that's interesting. Show me," booms God.

So the scientist bends down to the earth and starts to breathe on the soil.

"Oi!" says God. "Get your own dirt."

Be sure your sins will find you out

A man spent days looking for his wallet. Finally, he decided that he'd go to church and steal one from one of the many jackets left in the cloakroom. The would-be thief went to church and sat at the back. The sermon was about the Ten Commandments, but instead of sneaking out he waited until the sermon was over and went to talk to the vicar.

"Father, I came here today to steal a wallet, but after hearing your sermon, I changed my mind."

The delighted man of God said, "Bless you, my son. Was it when I preached, 'Thou shall not steal' that you had a change of heart?"

The man responded, "No, it was the one about adultery. When you started to preach about that, I suddenly remembered where I left my wallet."

In the number two shirt

Sven-Goran Eriksson walks into the changing room after a particularly vigorous training session – only to spot a steaming turd on the floor. Fuming, the Swede looks at his players and bawls, "Who's sh*t on the floor?"

"Me, boss," cries Peter Crouch, "but I'm not too bad in the air."

Out of the spotlight

How many Manchester City fans does it take to change a lightbulb?

None. They're quite happy living in the shadows.

Mug's game

What's the difference between an Argentine football fan and a bad cup of coffee?

Nothing; they're both bitter.

Kiss of life

A woman has been in a coma for several weeks, but one day nurses notice a slight response while washing her private parts. They rush to her husband and explain the surprise, suggesting a little oral sex might bring her round, to which he readily agrees. A few minutes later her monitor flatlines, showing no pulse or heart rate.

The nurses rush into the room crying, "What happened!?"

"I'm not sure," the husband replies sadly. "She may have choked."

Johnny cash

An English tourist walks into a New York drugstore and asks for a packet of condoms.

"Rubbers, eh?" says the chemist, recognising his customer is English. "That'll be ten dollars, including the tax."

"Jesus!" cries the Englishman. "Back home we just roll them on."

Long odds

A 90-year-old man says to his doctor, "I have an 18-year-old bride who's pregnant with my child. What do you think of that?" The doctor says, "I have an elderly friend who's a hunter. One day, when he was going out in a hurry, he accidentally picked up his umbrella instead of his gun. When he got to the field, he saw a rabbit sitting beside the stream. He raised his umbrella and went, 'Bang, bang' and the rabbit fell dead. What do you think of that?"

The 90-year-old says, "I'd say somebody else killed that rabbit."

The doctor replies, "My point exactly."

> **Do you know how copper wire was invented?**
> **Two lawyers were fighting over a penny.**

Thanks anyway

A man was walking down the street in a sweat because he had an important meeting and couldn't find a parking space. Looking up towards Heaven he said, "Lord, take pity on me. If you can find me a parking space, I'll go to church every Sunday for the rest of my life and give up lager." Miraculously, a parking space appeared.

The man looked up to Heaven again and said, "Never mind – I found one."

The beautiful game

Halfway through the first half of a school football game, the coach calls one of his nine-year-old players aside and asks, "Do you understand what co-operation is? What a team is?"

The little boy nods in the affirmative.

"Do you understand that what matters is whether we win or lose together as a team?" demands the coach.

The little boy nods.

"So," the coach continues, "I'm sure you know, when you're called offside, you shouldn't argue, swear, attack the ref or call him an idiot. Do you understand all that?"

Again the little boy nods.

The coach continues, "And when I take you off so another boy gets a chance to play, it's not good sportsmanship to call your coach a tw★t, is it?"

Again the little boy agrees.

"Good," says the coach. "Now go over there and explain all that to your dad."

Can't I just walk along a line?

A driver was pulled over by a policeman for speeding. As the officer was writing the ticket, he noticed several machetes in the car. "What are those for?" he asked suspiciously. "I'm a juggler," the man replied. "I use those in my act."

"Well, show me," the officer demanded.

The driver got out the machetes and started juggling them, eventually doing seven at one time. Seeing this, the driver of another car passing by said to his passenger, "Remind me never to drink and drive. Look at the test they're giving now."

Square meal

Two men went into a pub, ordered two beers, took some sandwiches out of their packs and started to eat them.

"You can't eat your own sandwiches in here," complained the pub-owner.

The two men stopped, looked at each other and then swapped their sandwiches.

Right back atcha

A guy returns home one day and says to his girlfriend, "Look, I've bought the new Oasis CD."

"Why did you do that?" the girlfriend laughs. "We don't even have a CD player!"

"So what?" says the chap.

"Have I ever asked why you keep buying bras?"

Applied psychology

A man bought a new fridge for his house. To get rid of his old fridge, he put it in the driveway and hung a sign on it saying: "Free to good home. You want it, you take it."

For three days the fridge sat there without even one person looking twice at it.

He eventually decided that people were too suspicious. It looked too good to be true. He changed the sign to read: "Fridge for sale, £50."

The next day someone stole it.

Gentle persuasion

How do you convince Jade Goody to go to bed with you?
  Piece of cake.

What's the difference between a waitress who works in a strip club and a stripper?
Two weeks.

Cry for help

Last night police were called to a branch of Pizza Hut after the body of a member of staff was found covered in mushrooms, onions, ham and cheese. The police spokesman said that there was a strong possibility that the man had topped himself.

Making dough

The owner of a family-run bakery was being questioned by the Inland Revenue about his tax return, having reported a net profit of £45,000 for the year.

"Why don't you people leave me alone?" the baker said. "I work like a dog, everyone in my family helps out and the place is only closed three days a year. And you want to know how I made £45,000?"

"It's not your income that bothers us," the taxman said. "It's these deductions. You listed six trips to Bermuda for you and your wife."

"Oh, that?" the owner said, smiling. "I forgot to tell you – we also deliver."

One size fits all

One day, two old ladies are sitting outside their nursing home having a cigarette when it starts to rain. One of the old ladies whips out a condom, cuts the end off, puts it over her cigarette and continues smoking.

Maude: "What the hell is that?"

Mabel: "A condom. This way my cigarette doesn't get wet."

Maude: "Where did you get it?"

Mabel: "You can get them at any chemist."

The next day, Maude hobbles down to her local pharmacy and announces to the chemist that she wants a box of condoms. Obviously embarrassed, he looks at her, but very delicately asks what brand she would prefer.

Maude: "Doesn't matter, as long as it fits on a Camel."

Holey communion

An old couple are sitting in church. After listening to the priest's sermon the old lady says to her husband, "I've just done a silent fart; what should I do?"

The old man replies: "Turn your bloody hearing aid up!"

Lagging behind

Two flies are in an airing cupboard. Which one's in the army?

The one on the tank.

Be safe, be seen

There is an accordion player driving home from a late-night gig. Feeling tired, he pulls into a service station for some coffee. While waiting to pay, he remembers that he locked his car doors but left the accordion in plain view on the back seat of his car! He rushes out only to realise that he is too late. The back window of his car was smashed and somebody had already thrown in two more accordions.

Heap big pun

An Indian chief had three wives, each of whom was pregnant. The first gave birth to a boy and the chief was so elated he built her a teepee made of deerhide. A few days later the second gave birth, also to a boy. The chief was very happy and he built her a teepee made of antelope hide. The third wife gave birth a few days later, but the chief kept the details a secret. He built this one a two-storey teepee, using hippopotamus hide. The chief then challenged the tribe to guess what had occurred. Many tried and failed. Finally, one young brave declared that the third wife gave birth to twin boys.

"Correct," said the chief. "How did you figure it out?"

The brave replied, "It's elementary, really – the value of the squaw of the hippopotamus is equal to the sons of the squaws of the other two hides."

And they're off!

Riding the favourite at Cheltenham, a jockey is well ahead of the field. Suddenly, he is hit on the head by a turkey and a string of sausages. He manages to stay on his mount and pull back into the lead, only to be struck by a box of Christmas crackers and a dozen mince pies over the last fence. He again manages to regain the lead when he's hit by a bottle of sherry full in the face. Eventually, he comes in second. Furious, he goes to the stewards' room to complain that he has been seriously hampered.

What's the punishment for bigamy?
Two mothers-in-law.

That's my boy!

Two old men are arguing about whose dog is smarter.

"My dog's practically a genius," the first fella boasts. "Every morning he waits patiently for the newspaper to be delivered and then brings it in to me."

"I know," the second fella replies.

"What do you mean?" the first man asks. "How do you know?"

The second man answers, "My dog told me about it."

Plain speaking

At one American university, students in the psychology class are attending their first lecture on emotional extremes.

"Just to establish some parameters," says the professor to a student from Arkansas, "what is the opposite of joy?"

"Sadness," replies the diligent student.

"And the opposite of depression?" he asks of a young lady from Oklahoma.

"Elation," she says.

"And you, sir," he says to a young man from Texas, "what about the opposite of woe?"

The Texan replies, "Sir, I believe that would be 'giddy up'."

Getting technical

One day at school, a teacher asks her class to write a sentence about a public servant, and little Jonny writes, "The fireman came down the ladder pregnant."

When she gets around to marking Jonny's answer, the teacher takes him aside to correct him. "Don't you know what pregnant means?" she asks.

"Sure," says Jonny. "It means carrying a child."

Bust-up

"My God! What happened to you?" the bartender asks Jim as he hobbles in on a crutch, one arm in a cast.

"I got in a fight with Steve Riley," he replies.

"Riley? He's your best mate and about half the size of you," the bartender says. "He must have had a weapon in his hand."

"Yeah. He had a shovel."

"Dear Lord. Didn't you have anything in your hands?"

"His wife's tits," Jim laments. "They're beautiful, but not much use in a fight."

A good man is hard to find

A middle-aged man and woman meet, fall in love and decide to get married. On their wedding night they settle into the bridal suite at their hotel and the bride says to her new groom, "Please promise to be gentle; I'm still a virgin."

The startled groom says, "How can that be? You've been married three times before."

The bride responds, "Well, you see, my first husband was a psychiatrist and all he ever wanted to do was talk about it.

"My second husband was a gynaecologist, and all he ever wanted to do was look at it.

"And my third husband was a stamp collector and all he ever wanted to do was... God, I miss him!"

A view to a quill

What's the difference between a porcupine and a pop star's tour bus?

The porcupine has the pricks on the outside.

Simmer on

There are two cowboys in the kitchen. Which is the real one?

The one on the range.

> **Why don't women blink during foreplay?**
> **They don't have time.**

Your sins are forgiven you

A nun goes to confession. "Forgive me, Father," she says. "I used horrible language this weekend."

"Go on," the priest says.

"Well," the nun continues, "I was playing golf and hit an incredible drive, but it hit a phone line and fell short after about only 100 yards."

"And you swore?" the priest asks.

"No," the nun says. "After that, a squirrel ran out and stole my ball."

"You swore then?" the priest asks. "Well, no," the nun says. "Then, an eagle swooped down and grabbed the squirrel in his talons. As they flew away, the squirrel dropped my ball."

"Then you swore?" the father asks.

"No," she continues. "The ball fell on a big rock, rolled on to the green and stopped six inches from the hole."

The priest is silent for a moment and then finally says, "You missed the f**king putt, didn't you?"

Bodily resurrection

A middle-aged woman has a heart attack and is taken to the hospital. While on the operating table she has a near-death experience. Seeing God, she asks: "Is my time up?"

God says, "No, you have another 43 years, two months and eight days to live."

Upon recovery, the woman decides to stay in the hospital and have a facelift, liposuction and a tummy tuck.

While crossing the street on her way home, she's killed by an ambulance. Arriving in front of God, she demands, "I thought you said I had another 40 years?"

God replies, "I didn't recognise you."

For God and country

A famous Welsh footballer died and upon arriving at the Pearly Gates was asked by the angel waiting for him, "Do you know of any reason why you should not enter the kingdom of Heaven?"

"Well," said the footballer, "once I was playing for Wales against England and I used my hand to push the ball past an English defender. The ref never saw it and I went on to score."

"Ah, that's OK," said the angel. "We can let you in."

"Oh, great!" replied the footballer. "That's been on my mind for ages. Thanks, Saint Peter!"

"That's OK," said the angel. "Oh, and by the way, boyo, Saint Peter's off today – I'm Saint David."

A lucky escape

A man walks into a bar grinning his face off. "The beers are on me!" he says, happily. "My wife has just run off with my best friend."

"That's a shame," says the barman. "Why aren't you sad?"

"Sad?" asks the man. "They've saved me a fortune. They were both pregnant."

Leaf well alone

Two caterpillars are sitting on a leaf when a butterfly flutters past them.

One caterpillar turns to the other and says, "You'd never get me up in one of those."

Double trouble

Two girlfriends are having a conversation about their boyfriends.

The first one says: "My boyfriend said he fantasises about having a threesome."

The other replies, "Yeah; most men do. What did you tell him?"

"I said, 'Why would you want to piss off *two* women?'"

What do you call a large cloud that marries lots of smaller clouds?
A bigger mist.

Bums' rush

What's the difference between a proctologist and a barman?

A proctologist looks at arseholes one at a time.

VIP treatment

The Pope lands in New York Airport, where a limo is waiting for him. The Pope gets in and says to the limo driver, "Mate, I haven't got a lot left in me. Please may I have an opportunity to drive a limo before I leave this world?" The limo driver thinks about it and agrees. The Pope then proceeds to drive the limo at 105mph down the streets of Manhattan until he's stopped by the police. The Pope winds down the window and gives the usual "Sorry, officer, I didn't know I was speeding" spiel. The cop gets on his radio and calls head office.

"I've pulled over a limo for speeding and it's got a very important passenger," says the cop.

"Who is it? The senator? The president?" asks the commissioner.

"No, much more important than that," replies the cop.

"Who's more important than the president?" scoffs the commissioner.

"I think it's God," says the cop.

"How could it possibly be God, you fool?" asks the commissioner.

"Well," replies the cop. "The Pope is the chauffeur."

I'll rephrase that

Two American women, one from the north and one from the deep south, are seated next to one another on a plane.

"Where you flyin' to?" asks the redneck, to which the northern woman turns up her nose.

"Don't you know you should never end a sentence with a preposition?" she says. The southern woman thinks about this for a second.

"OK, where you flyin' to, bitch?"

Where your money goes

While flying to South Africa, a plane crashes in desolate mountain terrain. The only survivor is an elderly lady who manages to stumble out of the wreckage. After crawling, hungry and exhausted, for several miles she finds shelter in a cave. After some time a Red Cross search party arrives, and begins crossing the mountain range looking for survivors. After a few hours they spot the cave entrance. "Is anyone alive in there?" shouts the group leader.

"Who's that?" shouts the old lady.

"Red Cross!" answers the leader.

"Jesus, you guys get everywhere!" shouts the old dear. "I've already donated."

Lucky escape

Two men are robbing a hotel.

"I hear sirens. Jump!" says the first one.

"But we're on the 13th floor!" his fellow-thief replies.

"This is no time to be superstitious!"

For whom the bells toll

Twelve priests were about to be ordained. The final test was for them to line up in a row, totally nude, while a sexy, big breasted model danced before them. Each priest had a small bell attached to their penis and were told that anyone whose bell rang would not be ordained because he had not reached a state of spiritual purity. Eventually, the beautiful model danced before the first candidate, with no reaction. She proceeded down the line with the same response from all the priests until she got to the final priest, called Carlos. As she danced, his bell began to ring so loudly that it flew off and fell clattering to the ground. Embarrassed, Carlos took a few steps forward and bent over to pick it up. Then, all at once, the other bells started to ring.

Bloody nuisance

Two nuns are driving down a road late at night when a vampire jumps on to the bonnet.

The nun who is driving says to the other, "Quick! Show him your cross."

So the other nun leans out of the window and shouts, "Get off our f*cking car!"

What did the German clockmaker say to the clock that only went, "Tick, tick, tick"?
"Ve haff vays of making you tock!"

Quick thinking

Resolving to surprise her husband, an executive's wife stops by his office. When she opens the door, she finds him with his secretary sitting in his lap.

Without hesitating, he dictates, "...and in conclusion, gentlemen, budget cuts or no budget cuts, I cannot continue to operate this office with just one chair."

The painful truth

A man goes to the dentist and asks how much it is for a tooth extraction. "£85 for an extraction, sir," was the dentist's reply.

"Have you not got anything cheaper?" replied the man, getting agitated. "But that's the normal charge for an extraction, sir," said the dentist. "What if I don't use any anaesthetic?" asked the man, hopefully. "Well, it's highly unusual, sir, but if that's what you want, I suppose I can do it for £60," said the dentist. "Hmm, what about if you used one of your dental trainees and still without any anaesthetic?" asked the man.

"Well, it's possible, but it'll be a lot more painful. If that was the case we could bring the price down to, say, £30," said the dentist.

"What if you use it as part of a student training session?" the man asked. "Hmm, well, OK...it'll be good for the students, I suppose. I'll charge you only £5 in that case," said the dentist. "OK, now you're talking. It's a deal!" said the man. "Can you confirm an appointment next Tuesday for the wife?"

It's a free country

A man phones up his local building firm and says: "I want a skip outside my house."

"Go ahead; I'm not stopping you," the builder replies.

Penne for your thoughts

A man and woman go on a date to an Italian restaurant. They arrive, order and the woman disappears to the toilet. The man waits for five minutes but there's still no sign of the woman. He is still waiting for her 20 minutes later when the food has arrived.

Finally, after half an hour she eventually comes back to find the man squeezing the pasta on his plate.

"What on earth do you think you are doing!" she screams in disgust.

"I was feeling cannelloni," he replies.

I confess

Henry goes to confession and says, "Bless me, Father, for I have sinned. Last night I was with seven different women." The priest quietly replies, "Take seven lemons, squeeze them into a glass and drink the juice without pausing."

Henry, looking surprised, says, "Will that cleanse me of my sins, Father?"

"No," says the priest. "But it'll wipe that stupid grin off your face."

Now you see it...

A young magician got a job working on a cruise ship with his pet parrot. The parrot would always ruin his act by saying things like, "He has a card up his sleeve," or "He has a dove in his pocket." One day the ship sank and the magician and the parrot found themselves alone on a lifeboat. For a couple of days, they just sat there looking at each other. Finally, the parrot broke the silence and said, "OK, I give up. What did you do with the ship?"

What did the mother turkey say to her disobedient children?
"If your father could see you now, he'd turn in his gravy."

Say it with flowers

A woman sent flowers to someone who was moving to Spain for a job promotion. She also sent flowers the same day to a funeral for a friend. Later, she found that the flower shop had got the cards mixed up. The man who was moving received the card that said, "Deepest condolences," and the card they sent to the funeral home said, "I know it's hot where you're going, but you deserve it."

The right career move

A plumber attended to a leaking tap at a stately home. After a two-minute job, he demanded £75. "Christ, even I don't charge this much and I'm a surgeon!" said the owner. The plumber replied, "You're right – that's why I switched from surgery to plumbing."

My heart won't go on

A Liverpool fan, a Man U fan and a Chelsea fan find
themselves waiting outside the pearly gates.

Eventually, St Peter emerges and informs them that in order
to get into heaven, they'll each have to answer one question. St
Peter turns to the Scouser first.

"What was the name of the ship that crashed into the
iceberg? They made a movie about it."

The Liverpudlian answers quickly, "That would be Titanic."

St Peter lets him through the gates.

He then turns to the United supporter and asks: "How many
people died on the ship?" Fortunately, the Manc has just seen
the DVD.

"1,228," he answers.

"That's right! You may enter."

St Peter then turns to the Chelsea fan. "Name them."

Doggy-style

What should you do if a Rottweiler starts shagging your leg?

Fake an orgasm.

Chaos theory

A doctor, an engineer, a vicar and a Royal Mail postman were
debating who was the world's first professional. The doctor
said, "It must have been a doctor. Who else could have helped
with the world's first surgery of taking a rib from Adam to
make Eve, the first woman?"

"No," said the vicar. "It must have been a rabbi, since the

Lord needed someone to help preach his message to Adam and the world."

"Wait," said the engineer. "The world was created in six days from nothing. Do you know what a master engineering feat that must have been to create the whole world into an organised, civilised place from utter chaos?"

"Yes, but who created the chaos?" asked the Royal Mail man.

Only trying to help

One winter morning an old couple, Norman and Sarah, are listening to the radio over breakfast. The announcer says, "We're going to have eight to ten inches of snow today. You must park your car on the even-numbered side of the street, so the snow ploughs can get through."

Norman's wife goes out and moves her car.

A week later while they are eating breakfast, the radio announcer says, "We're expecting ten to twelve inches of snow today. You must park your car on the odd-numbered side of the street, so the snow ploughs can get through."

Norman's wife dutifully goes out and moves her car again.

The next week again they're having breakfast, when the radio announcer says: "We're expecting twelve to fourteen inches of snow today. You must park..." Then the power goes out. Norman's wife is very upset, and with a worried look on her face she says, "Honey, I don't know what to do. Which side of the street do I need to park on so the snow plough can get through?"

With love and understanding in his voice, Norman says, "Why don't you just leave it in the garage this time, dear?"

Nuts

> **Why do police have trouble solving murders by rednecks?**
> **Because they all have the same DNA.**

Miracles take a little longer

A man walking along a beach is deep in prayer. Suddenly, the sky clouds over, and in a booming voice the Lord says, "Because you have been so faithful to me, I will grant you one wish."

The man says, "Build a bridge from my home in Manchester to the Greek islands, so whenever I want a holiday I can just drive there."

The Lord says, "Your request is very selfish. Think of the supports required to reach the bottom of the sea: the concrete and steel it would take: the destruction to the environment and the havoc caused to shipping lanes. Your bridge will nearly exhaust all of the world's natural resources. Take a little more time and think of something else."

The man says: "OK Lord, you're right, I'm sorry I was thoughtless. I wish I could understand my wife: how she feels inside: why she cries."

The Lord replies, "So, do you want two lanes or four on that bridge, then?"

Taking a dive

One day, a diver is enjoying the aquatic world 20 feet below the sea's surface when he notices a bloke at the same depth, but with no scuba gear whatsoever. The diver goes down another 20 feet and, after a few minutes, the bloke joins him. The diver goes down 25 feet more and, minutes later, the same bloke joins him again. This confuses the diver, so he takes out a waterproof chalkboard set and writes, "How the hell are you able to stay this deep under water without breathing apparatus?"

The other guy grabs the board, erases what the diver has written, and scribbles, "I'm drowning, you bloody moron!"

Crazy, man

What do you call a hippy's wife?

Mississippi.

A helping hand

The Prime Minister was out walking on a beautiful snowy day, when he saw that somebody had urinated on the Downing Street lawn to spell out "The PM is a d*ckhead." Infuriated, he called on the secret service to figure out who had done it. In a few hours, they came to him and told him that there was some bad news and some worse news.

"The bad news is that the urine is from the Chancellor."

"Al? How could he do this to me? What could be worse than this?"

"The handwriting is your wife's."

Only resting

What do you call a long line of actors?

A dole queue.

It's in the bag

A cowboy walks into a bar and orders a whiskey. When the bartender delivers the drink, the cowboy asks, "Where is everybody?" The bartender replies, "They've gone to the hanging."

"Hanging? Who are they hanging?"

"Brown Paper Pete," the bartender replies. "What kind of a name is that?" the cowboy asks. "Well," says the bartender. "He wears a brown paper hat, brown paper shirt, brown paper trousers and brown paper shoes." "How bizarre," says the cowboy. "What are they hanging him for?" "Rustling," says the bartender.

Chump, chomp, champ

A Russian and an American wrestler make it to the final at the Olympics. Before the pair contest the gold medal, the American wrestler's trainer comes up to him and says, "Now, don't forget all the research we've done on this Russian. He's never lost a match because of this 'pretzel' hold he has. Whatever you do, don't let him get you in this hold! If he does, you're finished!"

The wrestler nods in agreement. As the match begins, the American and the Russian circle each other several times looking for an opening. All of a sudden the Russian lunges forward, grabs the American and wraps him up in the dreaded pretzel hold.

A sigh of disappointment goes up from the crowd, and the trainer buries his face in his hands.

Suddenly there is a horrible scream, and the crowd cheers.

The trainer raises his head just in time to see the Russian flying up in the air. The Russian's back hits the mat with a thud, and the American weakly collapses on top of him, gets the pin and wins the match.

The trainer is astounded. When he finally gets the American wrestler alone, he asks, "How did you ever get out of that hold? No one has ever done it before!"

The wrestler answers, "Well, I was ready to give up when he got me in that hold, but at the last moment, I opened my eyes and saw this pair of balls right in front of my face. I thought I had nothing to lose, so with my last ounce of strength I stretched out my neck and bit those babies just as hard as I could. You'd be amazed how strong you get when you bite your own balls!"

What is it that separates five nymphomaniacs from two drunks? The cockpit door.

Bang to rights

What's the biggest crime committed by transvestites?
  Male fraud.

Sad but true

Why do elephants drink?
  To forget.

The simple answer

A boy comes home from school and says to his dad, "Dad, what's the difference between 'potentially' and 'realistically'?" His dad says, "Son, go and ask your mum if she'll sleep with Robert Redford for one million pounds, then go and ask your sister if she'll sleep with Brad Pitt for one million pounds." The boy says to his mum, "Mum, would you sleep with Robert Redford for one million pounds?"

"Definitely," she replies. He then says to his sister, "Sarah, would you sleep with Brad Pitt for one million pounds?"

"Definitely," she replies. The boy then returns to his dad, who says, "Did you find out the difference?" The boy replies, "Yes, potentially we are sitting on two million quid, realistically we are living with a couple of slappers."

Sweet sounds

How does Bob Marley like his donuts?
   "We' jammin."

Paper asset

What do accountants do when they're constipated?
   Work it out with a pencil.

Shall we gather at the river?

A drunk is stumbling through the woods when he comes across a preacher baptising people in the river. He walks down to the water's edge, then trips and falls before the holy man.

   Almost overcome by the smell of alcohol, the preacher pipes

up: "Lord have mercy on your drunken soul, brother; are you ready to find Jesus?"

Out of his skull, the drunk agrees: "Yes, I am!"

And with that, the preacher grabs him and dunks him under the water.

Moments later, he drags the boozer back up: "Brother, have you found Jesus?"

"No, preacher," stammers the drunk, "I have not!"

Stunned by this, the preacher sends the drunk down again... this time leaving him a little longer.

Finally he drags him back up again: "Rid your soul of the poison, brother; have you found Jesus?"

Gasping for air, the drunk splutters a reply: "No, preacher; I have not!"

At his wits' end, the preacher sends the drunk down one last time.

A full minute later, he pulls him out: "For the love of God," shouts the preacher, "tell me you've found Jesus!"

Coughing his lungs up, the drunk wipes his eyes and turns to the preacher: "You sure this is where he fell in?"

Banned substances

The ambitious coach of a girls' athletics team starts giving his squad steroids. Their performance soars, and they go on to win the county and national championships. The day after the nationals, Penelope, a 16-year-old hurdler, comes into his office.

"I have a problem," she says, "Hair's starting to grow on my chest."

"Oh my God!" yells the coach. "How far down does it go?"

"Down to my balls," she replies.

It's a family affair

One Sunday morning, George burst into the living room and said, "Dad! Mum! I have some great news for you! I am getting married to the most beautiful girl in town, and her name is Susan." After dinner, George's dad took him aside.

"Son, I have to talk with you. Your mother and I have been married 30 years and she's a wonderful wife... but she has never offered much excitement in the bedroom, so I used to fool around with other women a lot. Susan is actually your half-sister, and I'm afraid you can't marry her."

George was broken-hearted. After eight months, he eventually started dating girls again. A year later he came home and very proudly announced, "Diane said yes! We're getting married in June." Again, his father insisted on another private conversation, and broke the sad news: "Diane is your half-sister too, George. I'm awfully sorry about this." George was livid! He finally decided to tell his mother the truth about his father. "Dad has done so much harm. I guess I'm never going to get married," he complained. "Every time I fall in love, Dad tells me the girl is my half-sister."

"Don't worry about that," his mother chuckled, shaking her head. "He's not really your father."

Why do Rover cars have heated rear windows?
To keep your hands warm while you're pushing.

Getting results

A man calls a local hospital.

"Hello. Could you connect me to the person who gives information about patients? I'd like to find out if a patient is getting better, doing as expected or getting worse," he says.

The voice on the other end says, "What is the patient's name and room number?"

"Brian Johnson, room 302," says the man.

"I'll connect you with the nursing station," says the receptionist.

After a brief pause, the man hears: "3-A Nursing Station. How can I help you?"

"I'd like to know the condition of Brian Johnson in room 302," says the man.

"Just a moment. Let me look at his records... Mr Johnson is doing very well. In fact, he's had two full meals, his blood pressure is fine, he's to be taken off the heart monitor in a couple of hours and, if he continues this improvement, Dr. Cohen is going to send him home Tuesday at noon."

The man says, "What a relief! Oh, that's fantastic... that's wonderful news!"

The nurse says, "Are you are a family member or a close friend?"

"Neither! I'm Brian Johnson in 302! Nobody here tells me jack shit."

Word of command

What did the sign in the vet's waiting room say?

Sit! Stay!

Mission accomplished

A man was knocking back the drinks in a bar. "I think you've had enough, mate," said the barman. "But I've just lost my wife," slurred the drunk indignantly. The barman said sympathetically: "Well, it must be hard losing a wife." The man replied, "Hard? It was almost impossible."

In greatest need

A man walks into a chemist and asks for a bottle of Viagra. The pharmacist eyes him suspiciously. "Do you have a prescription for that?" he asks.

"No," says the man, "but will this picture of my wife do?"

Some you win...

A big Texan cowboy stopped at a local restaurant after a day of drinking and roaming around in Mexico. While sipping his tequila, he noticed a sizzling, scrumptious-looking platter being served at the next table. Not only did it look good, but the smell was wonderful. He asked the waiter, "What is that you just served?" The waiter replied: "Ah, señor, you have excellent taste! Those are bull's testicles from the bullfight this morning. A delicacy! But there is only one serving per day. If you come early tomorrow and place your order, we will be sure to save you this delicacy!" The next morning, the cowboy returned, placed his order, and then that evening he was served the one and only portion of the special delicacy of the day. After a few bites, and inspecting the contents of his platter, he called to the waiter and said, "These are delicious, but they are

much, much smaller than the ones I saw you serve yesterday."
The waiter shrugged his shoulders and replied, "Si, señor.
Sometimes the bull wins."

Not on my job description

An old woman is on a plane and is getting increasingly worried
about the turbulence around her. She turns to the vicar next to
her and asks: "Reverend, you are a man of God. Why can't you
do something about this problem?"

"Lady," says the vicar. "I'm in sales, not management."

**What do you call an Aussie farmer with
a sheep under each arm?
A pimp.**

Lovers' guide

Little Johnny walks past his parents' room one night and sees
them making love. Puzzled, he asks his father about it the
next morning. "Why were you doing that to mummy last
night?"

His father replies, "Because mummy wants a baby."

The next night, Johnny spots mummy giving daddy a
blowjob and the next morning he asks his father, "Why was
mummy doing that to you last night?"

His father replies, "Because mummy wants a BMW."

The name escapes me

A man walks into a pub with his wife. His wife sits down while he orders drinks and a friend of his at the bar asks him where he's been.

"On holiday," he replies.

"Where on holiday?" his friend asks.

"Spain."

"Whereabouts in Spain?"

"Some little village on the coast."

"What's it called?"

"I forget. What's the name of that plant that grows up the sides of houses?"

"Ivy."

"That's it," he says. "Ivy, what's the name of the village we stayed at in Spain?"

Lost in translation

Two Mexicans have been lost in the desert for weeks. At death's door, they see a tree in the distance. As they get nearer, they see that it's draped with rasher upon rasher of bacon: smoked bacon, crispy bacon, juicy bacon, all sorts of bacon. "Hey, Pepe," says the first Mexican, "ees a bacon tree! We're saved!" So Pepe goes on ahead and runs up to the tree. As he gets to within five feet of it, he's gunned down in a hail of bullets. His friend drops down on the sand and yells across to the dying man: "Pepe! Pepe! Que pasa, hombre?" With his last breath Pepe calls out, "Ugh, run, amigo, run – ees not a bacon tree, ees a ham bush."

My body is a temple

A woman walks up to an old man sitting in a chair on his porch. "I couldn't help but notice how happy you look," she said. "What's your secret for a long, happy life?"

"I smoke three packs a day, drink a case of beer, eat fatty foods and never, ever exercise," he replied.

"Wow; that's amazing," she said, "How old are you?"

"Twenty-six."

Left high and dry

A large cup and two smaller ones go out for a meal at a posh restaurant. When the bill arrives, the small cups do a runner, leaving their pal to pay up.

A week later, the three are back and, once again, the large cup is left behind to settle the bill.

The waiter comes up to him, and says, "No offence, mate, but I think your two pals are taking you for a mug."

Be careful what you wish for

Two men were out fishing, when they found a lamp floating in the water. One of the men picked it up and rubbed it, and straight away a genie appeared from the lamp. Unfortunately, it was a very low-level genie, and could only grant one wish. The men thought for a few minutes and then wished for the entire lake to be made of the best beer in the world. With a flash the wish was granted. All of a sudden, one of the men got really angry.

"Dammit! Now we have to piss in the boat!"

Thin-skinned

A young polar bear walks up to his dad one day and asks: "Dad, am I a pure polar bear? You know, not part black bear or grizzly bear or anything?"

"Why no, son. You come from a long line of proud and strong polar bears. Why do you ask?"

"Because I'm f★★king cold."

Lapsed membership

Did you hear about the leper who was a gigolo?

His business was doing rather well until it fell apart.

A man goes to the zoo but when he arrives there's only a dog.
It was a shih-tzu.

An apple a day...

A young man asked an old rich man how he made his money. The old guy stroked his worsted wool vest and said, "Well, son, it was 1932 – the depth of the Great Depression. I was down to my last penny so I invested it in an apple. I spent the entire day polishing the apple and, at the end of the day, I sold it for two pence. The next morning, I invested those two pence in two apples. I spent the entire day polishing them and sold them at 5pm for 4p. I continued this system for a month, by the end of which I'd accumulated a fortune of

£1.35. Then my wife's father died and left us two million pounds."

Sense of perspective

A very successful lawyer parks his brand-new BMW in front of the office, ready to show it off to his colleagues. As he gets out, a truck comes along, too close to the kerb, and completely tears off the Beemer's driver's door.

The lawyer immediately grabs his mobile, dials 999, and in about five minutes a police car turns up. Before the cop has a chance to ask any questions, the lawyer starts screaming hysterically. The BMW, which he'd just picked up the day before, is now completely ruined and will never be the same, no matter how the body shop tries to make it new again.

After the lawyer finally winds down from his rant, the cop shakes his head in disgust. "I can't believe how materialistic you lawyers are," he says. "You're so focused on your possessions that you neglect the most important things in life."

"How can you say such a thing?" asks the lawyer.

The cop replies, "You sick sod; don't you even realise that your left arm's missing? It got ripped off when the truck hit you!"

"My God!" screams the lawyer. "Where's my Rolex?"

Saving himself

David Beckham walks into a pub. The landlord says, "Your usual, David?"

Beckham replies, "Yeah. Just a half, then I'm off."

Between ourselves

A man is staying at a hotel on a business trip and, feeling lonely, reaches for an escort girl's business card he'd taken from a phone box earlier. He rings the number and a sexy-sounding woman picks up the phone and says, "Hello?"

"Hello," he says. "I hear you give a great massage and I'd like you to come to my hotel room to give me one... no, wait; I'll be straight with you. I'm all alone and all I want is sex – and I'm talking some seriously kinky stuff. Whips, chains, the lot – how does that sound?"

"That sounds fair enough," says the woman, "but for an outside line you need to dial 9."

Watch what you eat

Two men are sitting in the doctor's office. The first man is holding his shoulder in pain, while the second man has ketchup in his hair, fried egg down the front of his shirt and two sausages sticking out of his pockets. After a while, the second man asks the other what happened. "My cat got stuck in a tree," the man says, gripping his arm. I went up after him and fell out. I think I've broken my shoulder. You?"

"Oh, it's nothing serious," the second man replies. "I'm just not eating properly."

It doesn't quite add up

A bank manager in America notices that one of his new cashiers lacks basic arithmetic skills. He calls the new man into his office. "Son, where did you say you studied finance again?" the manager asks.

"Yale, sir," the cashier replies.

"I see," says the bank manager, certain he must have pulled the wrong employee aside. "And what did you say your name was?"

"Yim Yohnson, sir," he replies.

What do you call a woman who works as hard as a man?
Lazy.

Turn a deaf ear

A policeman in a small town stopped a motorist who was speeding down the High Street. "But, officer," the man began, "I can explain."

"Quiet!" snapped the officer. "I'm going to let you spend the night in jail until the sergeant gets back."

"But, officer, I just wanted to say..."

"I said be quiet! You're going to jail!"

A few hours later the officer looked in on his prisoner and said, "Lucky for you, the sarge is at his daughter's wedding so he'll be in a good mood when he gets back."

"Don't count on it," answered the bloke in the cell. "I'm the groom."

Batman and rubbin'

Who has the easiest job in the English cricket squad?

The guy who removes the red ball marks from the bats.

It's a miracle!

An alien is visiting earth to research the local customs. After a while he returns to the mothership to share his knowledge with the other aliens. He gathers his fellow-ETs and tells of how he landed in a green and pleasant land called England and witnessed a religious ceremony.

"I went to a large green field shaped like a meteorite crater. Around the edges there were several thousand worshippers. Two priests walk to the centre of the field to a rectangular area and hammer six spears into the ground, three at each end. Then eleven more priests walk out, clad in white robes. Then two high priests wielding clubs walk to the centre and one of the other priests starts throwing a red orb at the ones with the clubs."

"Ooooh," replies the amazed alien throng collectively, "what happens next?"

"Well," says the explorer alien. "Then it begins to rain."

Record breaker

A man walks into a music store to buy an old-school LP. As he gets ready to pay, he discovers that he has forgotten his wallet. But instead of running home to get it, he decides to steal the record by putting it down his pants. The cashier spots him on the way out and yells, "Hey! Is that a record in your pants?"

The man replies, "Well, I don't know if it's a record but I haven't heard of any complaints."

Q: How many men do you need for a Mafia funeral?
A: Just one. To slam the car boot shut

The greatest show on Earth

Why is marriage like a three-ring circus?

First there's the engagement ring, then there's the wedding ring, and then comes the suffering.

A first time for everything

A linguistics professor is lecturing his class.

"In English," he says, "a double negative forms a positive. However, in some languages, such as Russian, a double negative remains a negative. But there isn't a single language, not one, in which a double positive can express a negative."

A sarcastic voice from the back of the room replies, "Yeah: right."

> **How many drinkers does it take to change a light bulb?**
> **Never mind. We'll drink in the dark.**

It's enough to wake the dead!

A funeral service is being held for a woman who has just died. As the pallbearers are carrying out the casket, they accidentally bump into a wall. Hearing a faint moan from inside, the woman's husband opens the casket to find that his wife is actually alive! She dies again ten years later and her husband has to arrange another funeral. This time, when the casket is carried towards the door, the husband yells, "Watch out for the bloody wall!"

A fate worse than death

An Englishman, a Frenchman and a German survive a plane crash. They are stranded on a desert island and, knowing that nothing but certain death is to be their fate, God grants them one last wish. The Frenchman asks for a huge, sumptuous dinner washed down with an excellent Burgundy; the German asks if he can make the after-dinner speech; and the Englishman clasps his hands together and says: "Please, God, let me die before the German starts."

What was the question?

A man buys a 12 pack of condoms with his girlfriend and gets down to business straight away. A few days later, the two are at it again, and the woman realises that there are only three condoms left. A little confused, she confronts the man as to where the other condoms have gone. "I was masturbating," he replies. The girlfriend looks confused and says, "I've never heard of that." The next day she asks a male friend if he does the same, to which he replies, "Yeah, of course." The woman shrieks back, "Really? You've masturbated with a condom?"

The man looks surprised and says, "Oh no, sorry. I thought you said have I ever cheated on my girlfriend."

Holy orders

At the Gates of Heaven, God decides to put in a personal appearance and says, "I want the men to make two lines: one line for the men who were true heads of their households and the other line for the men who were dominated by their women. I want all the women to report to St. Peter."

Soon, the women are gone and there are two lines of men. The line of men who were dominated by their wives is 100 miles long, and in the line of men who truly were heads of their household, there is only one man.

God said, "You men should be ashamed of yourselves. I created you to be the head of your household. You have been disobedient and not fulfilled your purpose. I told you to be the spiritual leader in your family. Of all of you, only one obeyed. Learn from him! Tell them, my son; how did you manage to be the only one in this line?"

The man replies, "I don't know; my wife told me to stand here."

Nuts

Union mamba

How do you stop a snake from striking?

Pay it decent wages.

Honesty isn't always the best policy

Bob is sitting at the coffee shop, staring morosely into his cappuccino. Tom walks in and sits down. After trying to start a conversation several times and getting only distracted grunts, he asks Bob what the problem is.

"Well," says Bob, "I think I've upset my wife after she asked me one of those questions she always asks. Now I'm in deep trouble at home."

"What kind of question was it?"

"Well, my wife asked me if I would still love her when she was old, fat and ugly."

"That's easy," said Tom. "You just say, 'Of course I will!'"

"Yeah," said Bob, "that's what I did. Except I said, 'Of course I do'."

In the mean time

Two old Englishmen and two old Irishmen enter a bar and see a sign that reads, "Old Timers' Bar: All Drinks 50p!"

When the old bartender spots them he calls out: "Come on in and let me pour you a drink! What'll it be?"

The four men each ask for a martini and the bartender duly serves them up and says: "That'll be 50p each, please."

They pay for their drinks, down them and order another round. Again, four excellent martinis are produced for just 50p each.

The old men pay up, but their curiosity is too much and one of the Irishmen asks "How can you afford to serve martinis as good as these for just 50p a piece?"

"Here's my story," the barman says. "I used to be a tailor in London, but I always wanted to own a bar. Last year I hit the lottery for £15 million and decided to open this place. I think our culture is far too disrespectful to its senior members, so every drink costs 50p: wine, whiskey, beer, anything. Guys like you are coming from all over – it's great."

"Wow! That's quite a story," says one of the Englishmen.

The four of them continue drinking and can't help but notice three other blokes at the end of the bar who don't have a drink between them. In fact, they haven't ordered anything the whole time they've been there.

The Englishman gestures at the men and asks the generous landlord, "What's with them?"

The bartender says, "They're from Scotland. They're waiting for Happy Hour."

Why did the chicken cross the playground?
To get to the other slide.

Cereal crop

Why did the Cornishman plant Cheerios in his backyard?
He thought they were doughnut seeds.

Get it off your chest

An old couple were sitting on the porch one afternoon, rocking in their rocking chairs. All of a sudden, the old man reaches over and slaps his wife. "What was that for?" she asks. "That's for 40 years of rotten sex!" he replies. His wife doesn't say anything, and they start rocking again. All of a sudden, the old lady reaches over and slaps her husband hard across the face. "Well, what was that for?" he asks. "That's for knowing the difference!"

Fowl language

A young man's mother is now retired and living in Miami Beach. He doesn't see her that often. His father is no longer around and he is worried that his mum is lonely. For her birthday, he purchases a rare parrot, trained to speak seven languages. He has a courier deliver the bird to his dear old mother. A few days later, he calls to see that she got the bird. "Mum, what do you think of the parrot?"

"It was a little tough, actually. I should have cooked it longer," says the old dear.

"You ate the bird? Mum, that bird was really expensive. It spoke seven languages!" says the horrified son.

"Oh, excuse me! If the bird was so damn smart, why didn't it say something when I put it in the oven?"

Wise words

The teacher had given her class an assignment. She'd asked her pupils to get their parents to tell them a story that had a moral at the end of it. "So what have you got for me, Johnny?" she asks one pupil sitting at the back of the class.

"Well," replies Johnny. "My mum told a story about my dad. Dad was a pilot in Desert Storm, and his plane got hit. He had to bail out over enemy territory, and all he had was a small flask of whiskey, a pistol and a survival knife. He drank the whiskey on the way down, so it wouldn't fall into enemy hands, and then his parachute landed right in the middle of 20 enemy troops. He shot 15 of them with the gun, until he ran out of bullets, killed four more with the knife, until the blade broke, and then he killed the last one with his bare hands."

"Good heavens!" said the horrified teacher. "What kind of moral did your mum teach you from that horrible story?"

The boy replied: "Stay the hell away from Dad when he's been drinking."

Wrong number

A young man joins a big corporate empire as a trainee. On his very first day at work, he dials the canteen and shouts into the phone, "Get me a coffee, quickly!"

The voice from the other side responds, "You fool, you've dialled the wrong extension. Do you know who you're talking to?"

The trainee goes white and says, "No, who is it?"

The voice on the end of the line continues, "It's the company CEO."

The trainee thinks for a moment and shouts back, "And do you know who you're talking to, you fool?"

"No," replies the CEO, indignantly.

"Good," says the trainee, and slams down the phone.

One to tell the lads

A guy is shipwrecked on a celebrity cruise and wakes up stranded on a desert island with Kelly Brook. Anyway, after a few weeks they are having passionate sex. This is all fine and dandy for a bit, but the guy starts getting a bit depressed. Kelly comes up to him on the beach one day and asks, "What's the matter?"

"Well, it's wonderful," says the guy. "I'm on a tropical island with a beautiful woman, but... I miss my mates and going to the pub with them."

So Kelly replies, "Well, I'm an actress. Maybe if I get dressed in some of those male clothes which were left behind in the trunks, I can pretend to be one of your mates down the pub."

It sounded a bit weird but he thought he'd give it a try. So Kelly gets into the male clothing and they sit down next to each other. Then the guy goes, "Hey, Joe, you'll never guess who I've been shagging."

> **What do you get when you have 32 rednecks in a room?**
> **A full set of teeth.**

Payment in kind

A wife, frustrated by her husband's bone-idleness around the house in the DIY department, sees cause for concern one day when the toilet clogs up. She decides to ask if he'd mind seeing to it, and is greeted with a gruff, "What; do I look like a toilet cleaner?"

The next day the waste disposal unit seizes up. Summoning all her courage she says, "Sorry to bother you, dear. The waste disposal's broken – would you try to fix it for me?"

"What; do I look like a plumber? Get me a beer and sod off!" is the reply.

To cap it all, the next day the washing machine goes on the blink and, taking her life in her hands, the wife addresses the sofa-bound slob: "Darling, I know you're busy, but the washing machine's packed up."

"What; do I look like a bloody washing machine repairman?" her old man says.

Finally fed-up, she calls out three different repairmen to come and fix her appliances.

That evening, she informs her husband of this. He frowns angrily and asks, "So how much will it cost?"

"Well, they said I could pay them either by baking a cake or screwing them all," she says.

"What type of cake did they want?" he growls.

"What; do I look like Delia Smith?" she replies.

Chance in a vermilion

A sailor is driven off course by a storm, and smashes into a small island. The next morning, he awakes on the beach. The sand and sky are reddish. Walking around in a daze, the sailor sees red birds, red grass, red trees and red bananas. He is shocked to find that even his skin is red.

"Oh, no!" he exclaims. "I'm marooned!"

Trews I'm standing here

Why does Rupert the Bear wear checked trousers?
Because he doesn't have any fashion sense.

Frank confession

A young woman on a flight from New York to London asks the priest sitting beside her, "Father, may I ask a favour?"

"Of course, my child. What may I do for you?"

"Well, I bought an expensive woman's electronic hair dryer for my mother's birthday," says the female passenger. "The dryer is unopened and well over the Customs limits, and I'm afraid they'll confiscate it. Is there any way you could carry it through Customs for me? Under your robes perhaps?"

"I would love to help you, my dear," says the man of the cloth, "but I must warn you: I will not lie."

"With your honest face, Father, no one will question you," replies the woman.

When they reach the Customs area, the women lets the priest go ahead of her. The Customs official asks, "Father, do you have anything to declare?"

"From the top of my head down to my waist, I have nothing to declare," answers the priest.

"And what do you have to declare from your waist to the floor?" says the official.

"I have a marvellous instrument designed to be used on a woman, but which is, to date, unused."

Roaring with laughter, the official says, "Go ahead, Father. Next."

Thinking on your feet

A woman was having a passionate affair with an inspector from a pest-control company. One afternoon they were carrying on in the bedroom together when her husband arrived home quite unexpectedly. "Quick," said the woman to her lover. "Into the wardrobe!" And with that she pushed him into the wardrobe, stark naked. The husband, however, became suspicious and, after a search of the bedroom, discovered the man in the closet. "Who are you?" he asked him, with a snarl.

"I'm an inspector from Bugs-B-Gone," said the exterminator.

"What are you doing in there?" the husband asked.

"I'm investigating a complaint about moths," the man replied.

"So where are your clothes?" asked the husband. The man looked down at himself and said, "Those little bastards."

What was the last thing Nelson said to his men before they got on the boat?
"Get on the boat."

Steer hide

Why does a redneck's pulse race when he meets a woman wearing a leather skirt?

Because she smells like a new truck.

Nuts

Slow on the uptake

Two turtles are camping. After four days hiking, they realize they've left behind a bottle opener for their beer. The first turns to the second and says, "You've got to go back or else we've got no lager." "No way," says the second turtle. "By the time I get back you'll have eaten all the food."

The first turtle replies, "I promise I won't, OK? Just hurry."

Nine full days pass and there's still no sign of the second turtle, so the first finally cracks and digs into a sandwich. Suddenly the second turtle pops out from behind a rock and yells, "I knew it! I'm definitely not going now!"

Food for thought

Two best friends crash their plane in a desert. Ten days later, hunger finally gets to them. John pulls down his pants and says, "I am cutting my dick off so that I will have something to eat." "Think about your sexy wife," says Mike.

"Why the hell should I think about my wife?" blasts John.

"Well, I thought we might have enough meat for two if you thought about your wife," replies Mike.

Empathy

A priest, a doctor, and a lawyer are waiting one morning on a particularly slow group of golfers.

"What's wrong with these guys?" fumes the lawyer. "We must have been waiting for 15 minutes!"

"I don't know," say the doctor, "but I've never seen such ineptitude!"

"Here comes the greenkeeper," says the priest. "Let's have a word with him. Say, George, what's with that group ahead of us? They're rather slow, aren't they?"

"Oh, yes," says George, "That's the group of blind firemen. They lost their sight while saving our club last year. We let them play here any time free of charge!"

Everyone is silent for a moment.

Then the priest says, "That's so sad, I think I'll say a prayer for them tonight."

"And I'm going to contact my ophthalmologist buddy and see if there's anything he can do for them," the doctor adds.

"Why can't the selfish bastards damn well play at night?" asks the lawyer.

Kids say the funniest things

The teacher asked her students to use the word 'fascinate' in a sentence. Mary said, "My family and I went to London Zoo, and we saw all the animals. It was really fascinating."

The teacher said, "That was good, but I wanted the word 'fascinate'."

Sally raised her hand and said, "My family went to Chester Zoo and saw the animals. I was fascinated."

The teacher said, "Good, but I wanted the word 'fascinate'." Little Johnny raised his hand. The teacher hesitated because Johnny was noted for his bad language. She finally decided there was no way he could damage the word 'fascinate' so she called on him. Johnny said, "My sister has a sweater with ten buttons, but her tits are so massive she can only fasten eight."

Captain's innings

What is the height of optimism?

An English batsman applying sunscreen.

Crime of the century

A turtle is ambling down an alleyway when he's mugged by a gang of snails. A police detective comes to investigate and asks the turtle if he can explain what happened. The turtle looks at the detective with a confused look on his face and replies: "I don't know; it all happened so fast."

> "My wife is an angel."
> "Lucky you. Mine's still alive."

A worthy cause

A driver was stuck in a traffic jam. Suddenly, a man knocked on his window. The driver rolled down his window and asked, "What's up?" The man said excitedly, "President Bush has been kidnapped by terrorists. They will cover him in petrol and burn him if they don't get $10million ransom." The driver asked, "And what do you want me to do?" "Well, we're going from car to car and collecting for the cause," answered the man. "Aha... And how much are people giving?" asked the driver. "Oh, somewhere around one or two gallons."

Contain your excitement

A woman walks into a Mercedes dealership. She browses around, then spots the perfect car and walks over to inspect it. As she bends to feel the fine leather upholstery, a loud fart escapes. Very embarrassed, she looks around nervously to see if anyone has noticed her little accident and hopes a salesperson doesn't pop up right then. As she turns around, standing next to her is a salesman.

"Good day, Madam. How may we help you today?"

Very uncomfortably she asks, "Sir, what is the price of this lovely vehicle?"

He answers, "Madam, if you farted just touching it, you are going to sh*t yourself when I tell you the price."

Animal magnetism

What do you call a dog with brass balls and no hind legs?
    Sparky.

Baring their souls

While redecorating a church, three nuns become extremely hot and sweaty in their habits, so Mother Superior says, "Let's take our clothes off, and work naked."

The other two nuns disapprove, and ask, "What if someone sees us?"

But the Mother Superior says, "Don't worry; no one will see us. We'll just lock the door."

So the other nuns agree, strip down and return to work.

Suddenly, they hear a knock at the door, and grab their clothes in a panic.

Mother Superior runs to the door and calls through, "Who is it?"

"Blind man," a man's voice comes back.

So she opens the door, and lets in the blind man. He turns to the nuns and says, "Great tits, ladies. Now, where do you want these blinds?"

Two can play that game

Little Johnny and his grandfather have gone fishing. After a while, Grandpa gets thirsty and opens up his cooler for some beer. Little Johnny asks, "Grandpa, can I have some beer, too?"

"Can you stick your penis in your arsehole?" Grandpa asks back. "No." "Well, then you're not big enough."

Grandpa then takes out a cigarette and lights up. Little Johnny sees this and asks for a cigarette.

"Can you stick your penis in your arsehole?" Grandpa asks again. "No." "Well, then you're not big enough."

Little Johnny gets upset and pulls out some cookies. His grandfather says, "Hey, those cookies look good. Can I have some?" Little Johnny asks, "Can you stick your penis in your arsehole?" Grandpa looks at Johnny and senses his trick so he says, "Well, of course I can, I'm big enough." Little Johnny then says, "Well, go shag yourself, these are my cookies."

Did you hear about the dyslexic pimp? He bought a warehouse.

Sahara dessert

A man crawls out of the desert and into a small village, which has some market stalls in the street.

He crawls up to the first one. "Water: water! Give me water!" he cries.

"I'm sorry," says the first stallholder, "I only sell custard."

The man crawls up to the second stall. "Water: water! Give me water!" he cries.

"I'm sorry," says the second stallholder, "I only sell cream and sponge."

The man then crawls up to a third stall. "Water: water! Give me water!" he cries.

"I'm sorry," says the third stallholder, "I only sell hundreds and thousands."

"I can't believe no one has any water," says the parched man.

"I know," says the stallholder, "it is a trifle bazaar."

Wins... or not

A man is walking through the Sahara desert, desperate for water, when he sees something far off in the distance. Hoping to find water, he walked towards the image, only to find a little old man sitting at a card table with a bunch of neckties laid out on it. The man asks, "Please, I'm dying of thirst; can I have some water?"

The man replies, "I don't have any water, but why don't you buy a tie? Here's one that goes nicely with your ripped clothes."

The young guy shouts, "I don't want a tie, you idiot, I need water!"

"OK, don't buy a tie. But to show you what a nice guy I am, I'll tell you that over that hill there, about four miles, is a nice restaurant. Walk that way; they'll give you all the water you want."

The man thanked him and walked away towards the hill and eventually disappeared. Three hours later he came crawling back to where the man was sitting behind his card table. He said, "I told you: about four miles over that hill. Couldn't you find it?"

The young fella rasped, "I found it all right. They wouldn't let me in without a tie."

Speak up

Sarah hated Sunday School and always daydreamed. At school the teacher asks Sarah, "Who made the earth?" Will, who sits behind her, pokes her with a ruler to wake her up.

"God Almighty!" she shouts. "Correct," says the teacher.

"Who is the saviour of the earth?" asks the teacher. Will poked her again. "Jesus Christ!" she shouts. "Correct. And what did Eve say to Adam after their tenth child?" Will prangs her again and she shouts, "If you poke me with that one more time I'll snap it in half!"

Entrepreneur

The kids filed back into class Monday morning. Their weekend assignment was to sell something, then give a talk on salesmanship.

Little Mary led off. "I sold homemade biscuits and I made £30," she said proudly.

"Very good," said the teacher.

Little Sally was next. "I sold old magazines," she said, "I made £45."

"Very good, Sally," said the teacher.

Eventually, it was Little Mikey's turn. He walked to the front of the classroom and dumped a box full of cash on the teacher's desk. "£2,467," he said.

"How much!" cried the teacher, "What in the world were you selling?"

"Toothbrushes," said Little Mikey.

"Toothbrushes?" echoed the teacher, "How could you possibly sell enough toothbrushes to make that much money?"

"I found the busiest corner in town," said Little Mikey, "I set up a Dip & Chip stand. I gave everybody who walked by a free sample. They all said the same thing. 'Hey! This tastes just like dogsh*t!' Then I'd say, 'It is dogsh*t. Wanna buy a toothbrush?'"

A policeman got out of his car and the lad who was stopped for speeding rolled down his window. "I've been waiting for you all day," the policeman said.

"Yeah," replied the lad. "Well, I got here as fast as I could."

Last respects

Two guys are golfing on a course that is right next to a cemetery. After they tee off, one of the golfers notices that there is a funeral procession sombrely passing by. He takes off his hat, and places it over his heart. When the funeral is over, the other golfer asks, "Why did you do that?" The man replies, "Well, we were married for almost 40 years. It's the least I could do."

Who's the daddy?

Young Johnny was having nightmares, so his father, Dave, runs into his bedroom to wake him up. "Johnny, what's wrong?" Dave asks.

"I dreamt that Auntie Sue had died," the boy replies. The father reassures him that his favourite aunt is perfectly fine, but the next day, coincidentally, Aunt Sue dies. That night, Johnny has another dream – this time that his grandfather was dead. As before, Dave enters his room to wake him up. Dave again reassures him that Grandpa is fine, but on his way home, the boy's grandad is tragically run over by a bus. The next day, Johnny has another dream – just like before, the father asks what's wrong. This time, Johnny sobs, "I dreamt that my daddy had died."

So, the next day, Dave drives to work very slowly to avoid any accidents, eats nothing for fear of food poisoning and spends the whole day under his desk in case the roof caves in. When he gets home, his wife says to him, "You wouldn't believe the day I had – the milkman didn't come..."

Horse sense

On a farm lived a chicken and a horse, who loved playing together. One day, the horse fell into a bog and began to sink. So off the chicken ran to get help. Running around, he spied the farmer's new Harley motorbike. Finding the keys in the ignition, the chicken sped off with some rope, hoping he had time to save his friend's life. After tying one end to the rear of the bike, the chicken drove forward and, with the aid of the powerful bike, rescued the horse.

A few weeks later, the chicken fell into a mud pit and, soon, he too began to sink. The chicken cried out to the horse to save his life. The horse thought a moment, walked over and straddled the large puddle. He told the chicken to grab his 'thing' and he would lift him out. The chicken got a good grip with its beak and the horse pulled him up and out, saving his life. The moral of the story? When you're hung like a horse, you don't need a Harley to pick up chicks.

Life sentence

Why did God create Adam before Eve?

To give him a chance to speak.

In a class of its own

During the Ryder Cup in Ireland, Tiger Woods drives his BMW into a petrol station in a remote part of the Irish countryside. The aged attendant at the pump greets him and is completely unaware of who the golfing legend is.

"Hello, sir" says the attendant.

Tiger nods a quick "Hello" and bends forward to pick up the pump.

As he does so, two tees fall out of his shirt pocket on to the ground.

"What are they, then, son?" asks the attendant.

"They're called tees," replies Tiger.

"Well, what on earth are they for?" inquires the Irishman.

"They're for resting my balls on when I'm driving," says Tiger.

"Fantastic," says the Irishman, "Those BMW boys think of everything!"

That certain something

A young primary school teacher decides to teach her class a new word. She tells the class about her idea and asks if anyone can tell her a sentence using the word "definitely."

Little Sophie's hand shoots up confidently and she says: "The sky is definitely blue." "No, Sophie," says the teacher. "The sky is not definitely blue, it can be grey and cloudy.

Anyone else?" Callum's hand pops straight up and he proclaims: "The water is definitely clear." To which the teacher answers: "No, it's not, it can be blue or green." Then Craig, the shyest boy in the class, nervously raises his hand and asks: "If I fart, should it be lumpy?" "No," the teacher responds. So Craig says: "Then I've definitely crapped myself."

> **A man goes into the barbers. The barber asks, "Do you want a crew cut?" The man replies, "No, thanks, it's just for me."**

Thanks for nothing

A man is walking in the street when he hears a voice. "Stop! Stand still! If you take one more step, a brick will fall on your head and kill you."

The man stops and a big brick falls in front of him. The man is astonished. He walks on and after a while, he's going to cross the road.

Once again, the voice shouts, "Stop! Stand still! If you take one more step, a car will run over you and you will die."

The man does as he's instructed, just as a car come screeching around the corner, barely missing him.

"Where are you?" The man asks. "Who are you?"

"I am your guardian angel," the voice answers.

"Oh yeah?" the man asks. "And where the hell were you when I bought my Man City season ticket?"

A man's best friend

Howard comes home one evening to find his wife crying.

"What's the matter, darling?" he asks.

"I don't know what to do," she says. "I'd prepared a meal for a special night in, but the dog ate it."

"Don't worry, dear," he says. "I'll get us another dog."

Girl talk

A little girl is in line to see Santa. When it's her turn, she climbs up on Santa's lap. Santa asks, "What would you like Santa to bring you for Christmas?"

The little girl replies, "I want a Barbie and an Action Man."

Santa looks at the little girl for a moment and says, "I think Barbie comes with Ken."

"No," says the little girl. "She comes with Action Man – she fakes it with Ken."

Tail-ender

A guy goes into a doctor's surgery.

"Doctor, I've got a cricket ball stuck up my bum."

The doctor asks, "How's that?"

"Don't you start," the man replies.

Doing their bit

Due to a shortage of young men, a bear, a pig and a rabbit are summoned for National Service. While waiting for the medical examinations, they all admit they're terrified of being killed.

"I'm ungainly and pink," says the pig. "The enemy will see me a mile off – so I decided to chop off my tail." The rabbit nods sagely – and the bear realises the bunny's ears have been removed.

"I just hope it works," says the rabbit. Mystified, the bear watches as both animals enter the examination room – then return, smiling.

"We're free to go," says the rabbit. "They said a rabbit without ears isn't a proper rabbit, and a pig without a curly tail isn't a proper pig!"

He's about to leave with the pig when the bear pipes up.

"Hang on a minute!" he cries. "I'm massive and slow – I'd not last a day in combat."

The other two look at the bear.

"Well," says the rabbit, "your sharp teeth could be useful in combat. You might want them removed..."

Nodding miserably, the bear lies down – and the other animals start kicking his fangs out. Eventually, the dazed bear, blood pouring from his mouth, stumbles through the door. A moment later, he returns.

"Did you get let off?" asks the pig.

"Yesh," splutters the bear, "Apparently I'm too fat."

I have foreseen it

A worker rings up work and speaks to his boss: "Hi, boss, I'm sorry but I'm not going to be able to come in for work today." The boss replies by asking, "What's wrong with you?"

"I have a vision problem," explains the lad. "Sounds serious," says his boss. "What seems to be the problem?" "Well," says the worker, "I just don't see myself at work today."

We'll never know

An ugly man walks into his local with a big grin on his face.

"Why so happy?" asks the barman.

"Well, you know I live by a railway," replies the ugly man.

"On my way home last night I noticed a woman tied to the tracks. I, of course, freed her, took her back to mine and, to cut a long story short, we made love all night."

"You lucky sod!" says the barman. "Was she pretty?"

"Dunno... never found the head!"

What do you call a New Zealander with a sheep under one arm and a goat under the other?
Bisexual.

Stain on his character

At the Clintons' one morning, Hillary is reading the papers when she sees a story that Monica Lewinsky turns 31 years old that day. Not being able to resist a dig at her husband, she looks across at Bill over her cornflakes and says, "You know, it says here that Monica Lewinsky is 31 today."

"Oh, really?" replies an awkward Bill.

Not wanting to let her straying husband off the hook just yet, she gives him another dig. "She's certainly grown up fast, hasn't she, Bill?"

"Yes," says Bill, shooting her an irritated glance. "It seems like only yesterday she was crawling around the White House on her hands and knees."

Natural curiosity

What did the elephant say to the man?

"How do you breathe through that thing?"

Getting the job done

The CIA had an opening for an assassin. After all the interviews and tests, three candidates were left – two men and a woman. For the final test, CIA agents took one man to a door and gave him a gun. "We must know that you'll follow instructions, no matter what. Inside this room is your wife. Kill her." The man said, "I could never do that."

The agent said, "Then you're not the man for this job." The same thing happened with the second man. Finally, the woman is given the same instructions to kill her husband. She took the gun and went into the room. Shots were heard. Then screaming and banging on the walls. Then silence. Then the woman comes out, wiping sweat from her brow. "This gun was loaded with blanks," she said. "I had to beat him to death with the chair."

Hedging your bets

What do you say if someone tries to steal your gate?

Nothing; he might take a fence.

Apt pupil

A man calls his boss one morning and tells him that he's
staying home because he's not feeling well.

"What's the matter?" the boss asks.

"I have a bad case of Anal Glaucoma," the man says in a
weak voice.

"What the hell is Anal Glaucoma?"

"I can't see my arse coming into work today."

Set your mind at rest

A doctor has been treating an 80-year-old woman for most of
her life. When the doctor retires, the patient's case files are
given to a new young doctor. At her first check-up with him he
studies the files and is amazed to find a prescription for birth
control pills.

"Mrs. Smith, do you realise you're taking birth control pills?"
says the young doc.

"Yes; they help me sleep at night," says Mrs. Smith.

"Mrs. Smith, I assure you there is absolutely nothing in these
that could possible help you sleep," he says.

The old dear reaches out and pats the young doctor's knee.
"Yes, dear, I know that: but every morning, I grind one up
and mix it in the glass of orange juice that my 16-year-old
granddaughter drinks and, believe me, it helps me sleep at night."

The long arm of the law

The SAS, the Parachute Regiment and the Police go on a
survival weekend to see who's the best. After basic exercises,

the trainer sets them their next task – to catch a rabbit for supper. First up, the SAS. Infrared goggles on, they drop to the ground and crawl into the woods. They emerge with a rabbit shot clean between the eyes. "Excellent," says the trainer. Next up, the Paras. They finish their cans of lager, smear on camouflage cream and go. They eventually emerge with the charred remains of a rabbit. "A bit messy, but well done," says the trainer.

Lastly, in go the Police, walking slowly, hands behind backs. After an eternity they emerge with a squirrel in handcuffs.

"Are you taking the mickey?" asks the trainer. The police team leader nudges the squirrel, who squeaks: "Alright! Alright! I'm a friggin' rabbit!"

> **Two lawyers are walking down the street, when a beautiful woman walks by. "Boy, I'd like to screw her," says one lawyer.**
> **"Yeah, I would, too," says the other. "But out of what?"**

Potty mouth

Snoop Dogg is minding his baby son when, suddenly, the baby gargles, "Mother..."

The doting gangsta rapper is overjoyed and shouts out: "Fo Shizzle! You just said half a word!"

Pulling the wool over your eyes

A ventriloquist is visiting New Zealand when he stumbles across a small village and decides to have some fun. Approaching a man on his porch patting his dog, he says, "Can I talk to your dog?" The villager just laughs at him and says, "Are you stupid? The dog doesn't talk." "Are you sure?" asks the ventriloquist. Turning to the dog, he says: "Hello, mate, how's it going?"

"I'm doin' all right," the dog replies. At this, the villager looks shocked. "Is this your owner?"

"Yep," says the dog. "How does he treat you?" asks the ventriloquist. "Really well. He walks me twice a day, feeds me great food and takes me to the lake once a week to play."

"Mind if I talk to your horse?" the ventriloquist asks the villager. The horse tells the ventriloquist that he is also treated pretty well. "I am ridden regularly, brushed down often and kept in a nice barn."

"Mind if I talk to your sheep?" the ventriloquist then asks. In a panic, the villager turns around and shouts: "The sheep's a liar!"

Urbi et orbi

The Pope is taken sick and his trusted physician is summoned.

After examining the holy man for over an hour, the doc leaves the papal bedchamber and tells the assembled cardinals: "The bad news is that it's a rare disorder of the testicles. The good news is that all His Holiness has to do to cure himself is to have sex."

The cardinals argue about this diagnosis at length.

Finally they go to the Pope with the doctor and explain the situation.

After some thought, the Pope says, "I agree to this diagnosis, but under four conditions."

"What are the four conditions?" say the amazed cardinals.

"First the girl must be blind, so that she cannot see with whom she is having sex. Second, she must be deaf, so that she cannot hear with whom she is having sex. Third, she must be dumb so that if somehow she figures out with whom she is having sex, she can tell no one."

After another long pause the cardinals ask, "And the fourth condition?"

"She's got to have big tits," replies the Pope.

Mississippi yearning

A journalist goes to the Deep South to write a human interest story. Driving through the cotton fields, he spies an old farmhand and introduces himself.

"I was just wondering, Sir," the young hack asks. "Out here in the middle of nowhere – has anything ever happened that made you happy?"

The old timer replies, "One time my neighbour's sheep got lost. After forming a posse, we found it and then had sex with it before taking it home."

"Christ!" yelps the young man. "I can't print that!" After thinking for a second, the journo asks, "OK has anything ever happened around here that made you sad?"

The old man looks at the ground. "Well," he says sheepishly. "I got lost once."

Too good to be true

A man sinks his boat and ends up on a desert island. After about two hours, a beautiful blonde in a tight black leather catsuit walks up the beach. "Would you like a cigarette?" asks the blonde. "Yes, please," replies the shipwrecked man. With that, the blonde unbuttons her left breast pocket seductively and pulls out a packet of cigarettes and a lighter. The blonde then asks, "Would you like a drink?" "Yes, please," replies the man. With that, the blonde unbuttons her right breast pocket seductively and pulls out a large bottle of whiskey and a large bottle of brandy. The blonde then asks the man if he'd like to play around. The man looks surprised and replies, "Don't tell me you have a set of golf clubs in there as well."

What would life be like without women? A real pain in the arse.

Lower the undercarriage

A jumbo jet is just coming into the airport on its final approach. The pilot comes on the intercom, "This is your Captain. We're on our final descent. I want to thank you for flying with us today and I hope you enjoy your stay."

But he forgets to switch off the intercom. Now the whole plane can hear his conversation from the cockpit.

The co-pilot says to the pilot. "Well skipper, what are you going to do in town?"

Now all ears are listening to this conversation.

"Well," says the skipper, "first I'm going to check into the hotel and have a beer in the bar. Then I'm going take that new stewardess out for supper: you know, the one with the great legs. I'm going to wine and dine her, then take her back to my room for an all-night marathon session."

Everyone on the plane is trying to get a look at the new stewardess. Mortally embarrassed, she runs from the back of the plane to try and get to the cockpit to turn the intercom off. Halfway down the aisle, she trips over an old lady's bag and falls over.

The old lady leans down, pats her shoulder kindly and says: "No need to run, dear. He's going to have a beer first."

Boys will be boys

Two bored casino workers are working at the craps table. An attractive blonde woman arrives and bets $20,000 on a single roll of the dice. She says, "I hope you don't mind, but I feel much luckier when I'm completely nude." With that, she strips from the neck down, rolls the dice and yells, "Come on, baby, mama needs new clothes!" As the dice come to a stop, she jumps up and down and squeals... "Yes! Yes! I won! I won!" She hugs each of the dealers, then picks up her winnings and her clothes and quickly departs. The dealers stare at each other, dumbfounded. Finally, one of them asks, "What did she roll?" The other answers, "I don't know – I thought you were watching."

Moral: not all blondes are dumb, but all men are men.

Leafing so soon?

A nun, badly needing to use the toilet, walks into a local club.
The place is hopping with music and loud conversation and
every once in a while the lights turn off. Each time this
happens, the place erupts into cheers. However, when the
revellers spy the nun, the room goes dead silent.

"May I please use the ladies'?" the nun asks.

The bartender replies, "Sure: but I should warn you that
there's a statue of a naked man in there wearing only a fig
leaf."

"Well, in that case I'll just look the other way," says the nun.

After a few minutes the nun reappears, and the whole place
stops long enough to give the nun a loud round of applause.

The nun walks over to the bartender and says, "I don't
understand. Why did they applaud me just because I went to
the ladies'?"

"You see," laughs the bartender, "every time that fig leaf on
the statue's lifted up, the lights go out."

Immortal memory

An artist is summoned to paint a picture of General Custer's
last thoughts on the anniversary of his death. Two weeks later,
the artist comes back with a picture of a cow with a hole in it.
Through the hole, there are two Indians having sex.

The historical council is not pleased with the picture, so the
members ask the artist to explain the meaning of the picture.

The artist says, "It's simple. The meaning is this. 'Holy cow!
Look at the f*cking Indians!'"

It's the morning after the honeymoon and the wife says, "You know something, you really are a lousy lover." The husband replies, "How can you tell after only 30 seconds?"

Bird of pray

A priest walks into a pet shop to buy a bird. The owner beckons him over to a parrot. "This is a special parrot," he says. "If you pull the string on the left leg he recites The Lord's Prayer. Pull the string on his right leg and he recites Genesis." "What if you pull both strings?" asks the priest. The parrot screams: "Then I fall off my perch, you idiot!"

Wayside pulpit

A priest and vicar from the local parishes are standing by the side of the road holding up a sign that reads, "The end is near! Turn yourself around now before it's too late!"

They plan to hold up the sign to each passing car.

"Leave us alone, you religious nuts!" yells the first driver as he speeds by.

Seconds later the men of God hear screeching tyres and a big splash from around the corner.

"Do you think," says one clergyman to the other, "we should just put up a sign that says 'Bridge Out' instead?"

Nuts

Keep on running

A man was ordered by his doctor to lose 75lb due to serious health risks. Desperate, he signs up for a guaranteed weight loss programme. The next day a voluptuous 19-year-old girl arrives, dressed in nothing but running shoes and a sign round her neck, which reads, "If you can catch me, you can have me!" He chases her and after catching up, has his way with her. After a few days of this, he is delighted to find he has lost weight and orders a harder programme. The next day, an even sexier woman turns up, wearing nothing but running shoes and the same sign. After five days of her, he decides to go for the company's hardest programme. "Are you sure?" asks the representative on the phone. "This is our most rigorous programme." "Absolutely," he replies. The next day there's a knock at the door and standing there is a muscular guy wearing nothing but pink running shoes and a sign around his neck that reads, "If I catch you, you're mine."

Green with envy

A Catholic, a Protestant and a Mormon are sitting on a flight, talking about their families.

The Catholic says, "I have ten kids at home, and if I had another one I'd have a football team!"

"Well," says the Protestant, "I have 15 kids at home and if I had another one I'd have an American football team."

"Well," says the Mormon, "I have 17 wives at home." He pauses, sipping at his drink. "If I had another one, I'd have a golf course."

Fair point

A blonde was playing Trivial Pursuit one night. When her turn came she rolled the dice and landed on 'Science & Nature.'

Her question was:

"If you are in a vacuum and someone calls your name, can you hear it?"

She thought for a long while and then asked, "Is it on or off?"

Evening, officer

A policeman walks over to a parked car and asks the driver if the car is licensed.

"Of course it is," replies the driver.

"Great; I'll have a pint, then."

Grave situation

A man comes home from work to find his dog with the neighbour's pet rabbit in his mouth. The rabbit is dead and the man panics. He thinks the neighbours are going to hate him, so he takes the dirty, chewed-up rabbit into the house, gives it a bath, blow-dries its fur and puts it back into the neighbour's cage, hoping they'll think it died of natural causes. A few days later, the neighbour asks the guy, "Did you hear that Fluffy died?" The man stammers and says, "Um, no. What happened?" The neighbour replies, "We just found him dead in his cage one day, but the weird thing is that the day after we buried him, we went outside and someone had dug him up, given him a bath and put him back into the cage. There must be some really sick people out there!"

Oops...

A woman gets on a bus, and immediately becomes involved in an argument with the driver when he calls her baby ugly. She pays her fare and storms off to get a seat, visibly upset. The man next to her asks "What's the matter, love?"

"It's that bloody driver, I've never been so insulted in all my life," she replies.

"OK," says the man. "You go down there and sort him out. I'll look after the monkey."

> **Why are the English better lovers than the French?**
>
> **Because only an Englishman could stay on top for 90 minutes and still finish second.**

Suffering in silence

A pissed-off wife is complaining about her husband spending all his free time in the local boozer, so one night he takes her along with him.

"What'll you have?" he asks.

"Oh, I don't know: the same as you, I suppose," she replies, so the husband orders a couple of whiskies and throws his down in one shot.

His wife watches him, then takes a sip from her glass and immediately spits it out. "Yuck; that's terrible!" she splutters. "I don't know how you can drink this stuff!"

"Well, there you go," cries the husband. "And you think I'm out enjoying myself every night!"

Rigid with embarassment

Plucking up his courage, a young man goes to a notorious massage parlour for the first time. As he's not sure when to ask for the dirty deed, he lies on the bed, getting more and more aroused.

After a few minutes, the masseuse notices his condition. "Perhaps sir would like some relief?" she says breathlessly.

The man gulps. "Yes please," he stutters.

With that the lady leaves the room.

She returns a full fifteen minutes later. "Well," she says, popping her head around the door. "Finished?"

Wife support

A woman accompanied her husband to the doctor's office. After his check-up, the doctor called the wife into his office alone. He said, "Your husband is suffering from a very severe disease, combined with horrible stress. If you don't do the following, your husband will surely die. Each morning, fix him a healthy breakfast. Be pleasant, and make sure he is in a good mood. For lunch, make him a nutritious meal. Don't burden him with chores, as he will have had a hard day. Don't discuss your problems with him, it will only make his stress worse. And most importantly... make love with your husband several times a week. If you can do this for the next ten months to a year, I think your husband will regain his health completely." On the way home, the husband asked his wife, "What did the doctor say?" "You're going to die," she replied.

Master of all he surveys

How do you tell a male hippo from a female hippo?
  The male's the one with the remote.

Never look a gift horse in the mouth

A cop on horseback is at some traffic lights, and next to him is a kid on his bike. The cop says to the kid, "Nice bike you got there. Santa bring that for you?" The kid says, "Yeah." The cop says, "Tell Santa next year to put a back light on that bike." The kid says, "Nice horse you got there. Did Santa bring that for you?" The cop replies, "Yeah." The kid says, "Well, tell Santa next year to put the dick underneath the horse, instead of on top."

Nor the years condemn

Two men in their nineties have been friends for decades, and after going through the war together, they now just meet a few times a week to play cards. One day they're playing together when one of them suddenly puts down his cards. "Listen, don't get mad at me, pal," he says. "I know we've been friends for years, but I realised the other day that I can't remember your name. I'm really embarrassed but my memory is fading fast. Please remind me."

  For three minutes the other old fella just glares back at his mate, shaking his head. Finally, he stirs. "Look," he says, "how soon do you need to know?"

> **Woman: "Can I get Viagra here?"**
> **Pharmacist: "Yes."**
> **Woman: "Can I get it over the counter?"**
> **Pharmacist: "If you give me two of them, you can."**

Conflicting signals

During an interview for a points operator on the railway, the chief engineer asks a job candidate, "What would you do if the Plymouth-to-London was heading north on Track One and the London-to-Plymouth was heading south on Track One?"

"I'd definitely call my brother," the interviewee replies.

"Why on earth would you call your brother?" the chief engineer asks.

"Because he's never seen a train crash before," the applicant replies.

Hard to miss

A woman golfer comes running into the clubhouse in pain.

"Christ, what happened?" says the club pro.

"I got stung by a bee between the first and second holes," she replies.

"Hmmm," the pro murmurs. "Sounds like your stance was a little wide."

Money well spent

Two men standing in a bar have been drinking all day long. Both are heavily inebriated. The first man goes a bit green, then throws up all over himself. "Oh no, the wife's going to kill me; I promised I wouldn't drink today." His friend stops him short: "Don't you worry about a thing, pal. Place a ten-pound note in your jacket pocket and tell the missus some other guy hurled on you. Then the man put that money in your pocket to pay for the cleaning bill." The guy agrees and spends the rest of the day downing beers. On arriving home, his wife sees the mess he's in straight away and she asks: "Have you been drinking?"

"No, I certainly have not. Some other guy threw up on me and gave me a tenner for my troubles. Check in my jacket pocket if you don't believe me."

She checks. "But there's £20 in here." "Oh yeah, didn't I say? He sh*t my pants as well..."

Better luck next time

What's the difference between the Dutch World Cup squad and a tea bag?

The tea bag stays in the cup longer.

Unassailable logic

A rich lawyer is approached by a charity for a donation. The man from the charity is concerned that the lawyer makes over £1,000,000 a year but doesn't give a penny to good causes.

"First of all," says the lawyer, "my mother is sick and dying in the hospital, and it's not covered by insurance. Second, I have five kids through three divorced marriages. Third, my sister's husband suddenly died and she has no one to support her four children."

"I'm terribly sorry," says the charity man. "I feel bad about asking for money."

The lawyer responds, "Yeah; well, if I'm not giving them anything, why should you get any?"

A lot in common

It's a stockbroker's first day in prison and on meeting his psychotic-looking cellmate, the nutter notices how scared the stockbroker looks and decides to put him at ease.

"I'm in for a white-collar crime, too."

"Oh, really?" says the stockbroker, sighing with relief.

"Yes," says the cellmate, "I killed a vicar."

And the winner is...

A Greek and an Italian are arguing about whose culture has contributed most to the world. The Greek guy says, "Well, we have the Parthenon."

"We have the Colosseum," the Italian counters.

"We gave birth to advanced mathematics," the Greek retorts.

"But we built the Roman Empire," the Italian challenges.

Finally the Greek says triumphantly, "We invented sex!"

"That may be true," replies the Italian, "but we introduced it to women."

One morning A man phones up his work and says to his boss, "Sorry, but I can't come in today, I'm feeling a little sick."

The boss asks, "What do you mean 'a little sick'? Just how sick are you?"

The man replies, "Well, I've just had sex with my dog."

The ride of your life

What's the difference between a car tyre and 365 condoms?

One's a Goodyear, the other's a bloody great year.

Serving time

A woman awakens during the night to find that her husband is not in bed. She puts on her robe and goes downstairs to look for him. She finds him sitting at the kitchen table with a cup of coffee in front of him. He appears to be in deep thought, just staring at the wall. She watches as he wipes a tear from his eye and takes a sip of his coffee.

"What's the matter, dear?" she asks tenderly. "Why are you down here at this time of night?" The husband looks up.

"Do you remember when we were first dating, we were so young?" he asks. "Yes, I do," she replies. The husband continues, his voice brimming with emotion.

"Do you remember when your father caught us in the back

seat of my car making love?" "Yes, I remember," says the wife. The husband continues. "Do you remember when he shoved the shotgun in my face and said, 'Either you marry my daughter, or I'll see that you go to jail for 30 years'?"

"I remember that," she replies softly, taking his hand. He wipes a tear from his cheek and says, "I would have got out today."

First things first

A man and his wife walk into a dentist's office. The man says to the dentist, "Doc, I'm in one hell of a hurry! I have two mates sitting out in my car waiting for us to go and play golf, so forget about the anaesthetic and just pull the tooth and be done with it. We have a 10am tee time at the best golf course in town and it's 9:30 already. I don't have time to wait for the anaesthetic to work!"

The dentist thinks to himself, "My goodness; this is a brave man asking to have his tooth pulled without using anything to kill the pain." So the dentist asks him, "Which tooth is it, sir?"

The man turns to his wife and says, "Open your mouth and show him, dear."

Life sentence

A defence lawyer says to his client: "I've got good news and bad news. The bad news is your blood test came back and the DNA is an exact match with the sample found on the victim's shirt."

"Damn," says the client. "What's the good news?"

"Your cholesterol is down to 140."

Oh, I *see* ....

A keen golfer is taking lessons with a pro. "What should I do?" asks the man.

"Hold the club gently," the pro replies, "just like you'd hold your wife's breast." Taking the advice, he swings and blasts the ball 250 yards up the fairway.

Ecstatic, the man rushes home to tell his wife the good news. Upon hearing of his success, she books a lesson herself.

The next day the pro watches her swing and says, "No, no, no; you're gripping the club way too hard."

"What can I do?" asked the wife.

"Hold the club gently, just like you'd hold your husband's penis."

The wife listens carefully to the pro's advice, takes a swing, and the ball skips down the fairway no further than 15 feet.

"You know, that was a lot better than I expected," the pro says. "Now, take the club out of your mouth and try with your hands."

Scared stiff

A taxi passenger tapped the driver on the shoulder to ask him a question. The driver screamed, lost control of the car and stopped just centimetres from a shop window. The driver turned round and said, "Look, mate, don't do that again. You scared the daylights out of me!" The passenger apologized and said he didn't realise that a tap on the shoulder could scare the driver so much. The driver replied, "Sorry, it's not your fault, mate. Today is my first day as a cab driver – I've been driving hearses for the last 25 years."

Beastly business

A farmer wanted to have his hens 'serviced', and over a few ales in the local pub that night heard about a guy in the village who wanted to sell a rooster. The next day the farmer went to the man's house and bought the rooster. As he was leaving the guy shouted out, "Don't worry. That's the randiest bird you'll ever come across."

Sure enough, as soon as the farmer got the rooster into the yard it ran into the hen house and mounted each one in a flash. Then it ran into the barn and mounted all the horses. Then it went into the pig pen and did the same there.

The farmer tried to stop the rooster. "Stop!" he shouted. "You'll kill yourself!" But the rooster continued, seeking out each farm animal in turn.

The next morning the farmer looked out on the yard and saw the rooster, on his back with his legs in the air, and a buzzard hovering above. The farmer walked up to the rooster and said, "Look what you did. You killed yourself. Well, I did warn you."

Suddenly, the rooster opened an eye. "Shhhhh," it whispered. "That buzzard's getting closer."

A man asked a waiter: "I'm just wondering, exactly how do you prepare your chickens?"
"Nothing special, sir. We just tell them straight out that they're going to die."

How the other half lives

A priest and a nun are on their way back from the seminary when their car breaks down.

The garage doesn't open until morning, so they have to spend the night in a B&B. It only has one room available.

The priest says: "Sister, I don't think the Lord would object if we spend the night sharing this one room. I'll sleep on the sofa and you have the bed."

"I think that would be fine," agrees the nun. They prepare for bed, say some prayers and settle down to sleep.

Ten minutes pass, and the nun says: "Father, I'm very cold."

"OK," says the priest, "I'll get a blanket from the cupboard."

Another ten minutes pass and the nun says again: "Father, I'm still terribly cold."

The priest says: "Don't worry; I'll get up and fetch you another blanket."

Another ten minutes pass, then the nun murmurs softly: "Father, I'm still very cold. I don't think the Lord would mind if we acted as husband and wife just for a night."

"You're right," says the priest. "Get your own blankets, woman."

Why are women like hurricanes?
Because when they arrive they're warm, wet and wild, and when they go they take the house, the car... the whole f**king lot.

Divine intervention

A Catholic priest and a nun are enjoying a rare round of golf on their day off. The priest steps up to the first tee and takes a mighty swing. He misses the ball entirely and says, "Sh*t, I missed."

The good Sister demands that he watches his language: but on his next swing, he does it again and shouts, "Sh*t, I missed."

"Father, I'm not going to play with you if you keep swearing," the nun complains.

The priest promises to hold his tongue, but on the fourth tee he misses again, and can't stop cursing.

The Sister is really mad now and says, "Father John, God is going to strike you dead if you keep swearing like that."

On the next tee, Father John continues his bad form. Again he instinctively cries out, "Sh*t, I missed."

Suddenly a terrible rumble is heard and a gigantic bolt of lightning strikes Sister Marie dead in her tracks. Then, from the sky, a booming voice can be heard... "Sh*t, I missed!"

Happiest days of your life

The children had all been photographed, and the teacher was trying to persuade them each to buy a copy of the group picture.

"Just think how nice it will be to look at when you are all grown up and say, 'There's Jennifer; she's a lawyer,' or 'That's Michael; he's a doctor'."

A small voice at the back of the room rang out, "And there's the teacher. She's dead."

Here we go gathering nuts in May

Alan and his friend Martin went out hunting. Martin had never hunted before, so he was following Alan's lead. Alan saw a herd of deer and told Martin to stay in the exact spot he was and to be quiet. A moment later, Alan heard a scream. He ran back and asked Martin what had happened. "A snake slithered across my feet," said Martin, "but that didn't make me scream. Then a bear came up to me and snarled, but I still didn't scream."

"So why did you?" Alan asked, infuriated.

"Well," Martin went on, "two squirrels crawled up my trousers and I heard one of them say, 'Should we take 'em home or eat 'em now?'"

Robbie Williams and Emile Heskey are on a sinking ship. Who gets saved?
The music world and Birmingham City.

Tonic for the troops

The soldiers are tired and lonely after spending weeks in enemy territory. To entertain them the Major calls for a dancer from the nearby town to entertain them. After the first dance, the soldiers go mad, clapping for five minutes.

For her second number she strips and dances in a sheer bra and G-string. This time the applause goes on for ten minutes.

For her next number she dances topless, and this time the applause goes on and on. The Major has to come on stage and ask them to quieten down for the grand finale.

For her last number, she strips completely and dances naked. The Major expects the soldiers to make enough noise to bring the roof down, but ten minutes later, there is no clapping.

As the dancer comes offstage, the Major asks her, "What happened? How come there was no clapping this time?"

"How do you expect them to clap with one hand?" she says.

Only doing my job

The police chief was putting the new recruits through their paces and explaining to them how their new job might throw up some difficult issues. "For instance," he says, "what would you do if you had to arrest your wife's mother?"

One of the recruits raises his hand and says, "Call for back-up, sir."

Caught short

Two women walking home drunk need to pee, so they duck into a graveyard. They have no bog roll, so one woman uses her pants and throws them away. The other uses a ribbon from a wreath. The next day their husbands are talking.

"We'd better keep an eye on our wives," says one man. "Mine came home without her knickers." "You think that's bad," says the other man. "Mine had a card up her bum saying, 'From all the lads at the fire station, we'll never forget you'."

Jeux sans frontières

Why do the French never play hide-and-seek?

Nobody wants to look for them.

Somebody up there likes me

The Chief Rabbi challenges the Pope to a game of golf.

The Pope then meets with the College of Cardinals to discuss the proposal. "Your Holiness," says one of the Cardinals, "I am afraid that this would tarnish our image in the world. You're terrible at golf."

"Don't we have a Cardinal to represent me?" says the Pope.

"There is a man named Jack Nicklaus, an American golfer, who is a devout Catholic. We can arrange to make him a Cardinal, and then ask him to play as your personal representative," says the Cardinal.

Of course, Nicklaus is honoured, and he agrees to play as a representative of the Pope.

The day after the match, Nicklaus reports to the Vatican to inform the Pope of the result. "I have some good news and some bad news, Your Holiness," says Nicklaus.

"Tell me the good news, Cardinal Nicklaus," says the Pope.

"Well, Your Holiness, I don't like to brag, but even though I have played some terrific rounds of golf in my life, this was the best I have ever played, by far. I must have been inspired from above."

"How can there be bad news, then?" the Pope asks.

"I lost by three strokes to Rabbi Woods," replies Nicklaus.

Birthday blues

Two weeks ago was my 45th birthday. I wasn't feeling too good that morning, but as I walked into my office, my secretary Janet said, "Good morning, boss. Happy birthday." And I felt a little better that someone had remembered.

I worked until noon, then Janet knocked on my door and said, "You know, it's such a beautiful day outside, and it's your birthday, let's go to lunch, just you and me." We went to lunch. On the way back to the office, she said, "You know, it's such a beautiful day. Let's go to my apartment." After arriving at her apartment she said, "Boss, if you don't mind, I think I'll go into the bedroom and slip into something more comfortable." "Sure!" I excitedly replied. She went into the bedroom and, in a few minutes, returned carrying a huge birthday cake – followed by my wife, children and dozens of our friends, all singing Happy Birthday. And I just sat there – on the couch – naked.

> **What's brown and black and looks good on a lawyer?**
> **A doberman.**

Better safe than sorry

Japan has banned all animal transport after discovering some nibbled beds in Tokyo.

They think it could be a case of Futon Mouse.

Nuts

Three tough mice

Three mice were sitting at a bar talking about how tough they were. The first mouse slams a shot and says, "I play with mousetraps for fun. I'll run into one on purpose and as it's closing on me, I'll grab the bar and bench press it 20 to 30 times." The second mouse turns to him, slams a shot and says, "That's nothing. I take those poison bait tablets, cut them up and snort them, just for the fun of it." The third mouse turns to both of them, slams a shot, gets up and walks away and shouts, "I'm going home to shag the cat."

Bum steer

Three bulls, one large, one medium, and one small, are standing in the pasture. They've just heard a rumour that the farmer is bringing in a new, larger bull.

The largest bull of the three says, "Well, he ain't getting none of my cows."

The medium bull says, "He ain't getting none of my cows."

So the little bull says, "Well, if he ain't getting any of yours, then he sure as hell ain't getting one of mine."

Two days later, a truck pulls into the yard, and the farmer unloads the new bull. He's big and pissed off from having been cooped up for the long journey.

When the three bulls see him, the biggest bull says, "He can have my cows."

The medium bull says, "Yup, he can have mine, too."

The littlest bull, however, begins to paw the ground, snort and bellow.

"What the hell are you doing?" the other two ask.

"I'm just showing him I ain't a cow!"

Now, you might feel a little prick

Two little boys, Sammy and Tom, are sharing a room in hospital.

As they're getting to know each other, Sammy asks, "What're you in for?"

"I'm getting my tonsils out. I'm a little worried," says Tom.

"Oh, don't worry about it," Sammy says. "I had my tonsils out and it was brilliant! I got to eat all the ice cream and jelly I wanted for two weeks!"

"Oh, yeah?" replies Tom. "That's not half bad. Hey, Sammy; how about you? What're you here for?"

"I'm getting a circumcision, whatever that is," Sammy answers.

"Oh, my God, circumcision? I had one of those when I was a baby and I couldn't walk for a year!" says Tom.

Man says to God, "God, why did you make woman so beautiful?"

God says, "So you would love her."

"But, God," the man arrogantly asks, "why did you make her so dumb?"

God says, "So she would love you."

Clear my diary

When the new patient is settled comfortably on the couch, the psychiatrist begins his therapy session.

"I'm not aware of the nature of your problem," the doctor says, "so perhaps you should start at the very beginning."

"Of course," replies the patient. "In the beginning, I created the Heavens and the Earth."

I'm alright!

A young couple visit a marriage counsellor. The counsellor asks the wife what the problem is. She responds, "My husband suffers from premature ejaculation." The counsellor turns to her husband and enquires, "Is that true?" The husband replies, "Well, not exactly – it's her that suffers, not me."

How many psychiatrists does it take to change a light bulb?
Only one, but it really has to want to change.

Flights of fantasy

What do cookery books and science fiction have in common?

Men read them and think, "Well, that's not going to happen."

Employee relations manual

To cut costs, a managing director is forced to sack an employee. After much thought, he narrows the choice down to two young members off the office: Jack and Jill. As the pair have near-identical performance records, he cannot decide who should go, so, after hours of deliberation, he comes up with an idea; the first person to go for a fag break on Monday morning gets axed.

Monday arrives and Jill walks in with a monstrous hangover. After a few minutes, she heads outside for a cigarette. The director walks over. "Jill, I'm so sorry," he says, "but due to circumstances beyond my control, I've got to lay you or Jack off..."

"OK," replies Jill. "Would you just jack off, then? I've got a bloody awful headache this morning."

Many a slip

A man enters hospital for a circumcision. The surgeons lie him down, put him to sleep and set to work on the job in hand. When the man comes to after the procedure, he's perturbed to see several doctors standing around his bed.

"Son, there's been a bit of a mix-up," admits the surgeon. "I'm afraid there was an accident, and we were forced to perform a sex-change operation."

"What!" gasps the patient. "You mean I'll never experience another erection?"

"Oh, you might," the surgeon reassures him, "just not yours."

Looks like a vasectomy to me

After their 11th child a couple from Somerset decide that's
enough. The husband goes to his doctor and tells him that he
wants the snip.

"OK," says the doctor. "Go home, get a cherry bomb, light
it, put it in a beer can, then hold the can up to your ear and
count to 10."

The bumpkin replies, "I may not be the smartest man alive,
but I don't see how putting a cherry bomb in a beer can next
to my ear is going to help me."

So the man drives to London for a second opinion. The
London physician is just about to explain the procedure for
a vasectomy when he notices from the case file that the man
is from Somerset. Instead the doc says, "Go home and get a
cherry bomb, light it, place it in a beer can, hold it to your ear
and count to 10."

The bumpkin figures that both doctors can't be wrong, so he
goes home, lights a cherry bomb and puts it in a beer can. He
holds the can up to his ear and begins the countdown.

"1, 2, 3, 4, 5...", at which point he pauses, places the beer
can between his legs and resumes counting on his other hand.

Poultry and motion

Brian returns home from the pub late one night, stinking
drunk. He gets into bed with his sleeping wife, gives her a kiss
and nods off. When he awakes a strange man is standing at the
end of his bed in a long flowing white robe.

"Who the hell are you?" demands Brian. "What are you
doing in my bedroom?"

"This isn't your bedroom," the man answers, "and I'm St Peter".

Brian is stunned. "You mean I'm dead? That can't be; I have so much to live for! I haven't said goodbye to my family. You've got to send me back straight away!"

"Well you can be reincarnated," the holy man says, "but there's a catch. We can only send you back as a hen."

Brian's devastated, but knowing there's a farm near his house, he asks to be sent back right away. A flash of light later, he's covered in feathers and pecking the ground. Within minutes he feels a strange feeling welling up inside him.

The farmyard rooster strolls over and says: "I can see you're struggling, mate. Don't worry; you're ovulating. Just relax and let it happen. You'll feel much better." And so he does.

A few uncomfortable seconds later, an egg pops out from under his tail and an immense feeling of relief sweeps through him. When he lays his second egg, the feeling of happiness is overwhelming and he realises that being reincarnated as a hen is the best thing that has ever happened to him. The joy keeps coming but just as he's about to lay his third egg, he feels a massive smack on the back of his head and hears his wife shouting, "Brian, wake up you drunken b*stard! You're sh*tting the bed."

Why did the blonde take a ladder into the bar?
She heard the drinks were on the house.

Nuts

Easy when you know

A woman arrives at the gates of Heaven. While she's waiting for Saint Peter to greet her, she peeks through the gates. She sees a beautiful banqueting table. Sitting all around are her parents and all the other people she had loved and who had died before her.

When Saint Peter comes by, the woman says to him, "This is such a wonderful place! How do I get in?"

"You have to spell a word," Saint Peter told her.

"Which word?" the woman asks.

"Love."

The woman correctly spells 'Love' and Saint Peter welcomes her into Heaven.

About a year later, Saint Peter comes to the woman and asks her to watch the gates of Heaven for him that day. While the woman is guarding the gates, her husband arrives. "Darling, how have you been?" she asks.

"Oh, I've been doing pretty well since you died," her husband tells her. "I married the beautiful young nurse who took care of you while you were ill. We were on honeymoon and I went water-skiing. I fell and hit my head, and here I am. How do I get in?"

"You have to spell a word," the woman told him.

"Which word?" her husband asks.

"Antidisestablishmentarianism," she replies.

Third-rate performance

A woman meets a smart man in a bar. They talk and end up leaving together. Back at his flat, she notices his bedroom is packed with small teddy bears lined up all the way along the floor, medium-sized ones on a shelf a little higher, and enormous fluffy bears on the top shelf along the wall. The woman is surprised, but decides not to mention it as she is quite impressed by the man's sensitive side. After an intense night of passion, the woman rolls over and asks, "Tell me, how was it?" The man replies:

"Help yourself to any prize from the bottom shelf, love."

Meeting his match

A scientist is sharing a train carriage from Norfolk to London with a farmer. To pass the time, he decides to play a game with the farmer.

"I'll ask you a question and if you get it wrong, you have to pay me a pound," says the scientist arrogantly. "Then you ask me a question, and if I get it wrong, you get a tenner."

"You're on," says the farmer.

"OK; you go first," says the scientist.

The farmer thinks for a bit then says, "I know. What has three legs, takes ten hours to climb up a palm tree and ten seconds to get back down?"

The scientist is very confused and thinks long and hard about the question. Finally, the train is pulling into Waterloo. As it comes to a stop, the scientist takes out his tenner and gives it to the farmer.

"Well, you've got me stumped," says the scientist. "What does have three legs, takes ten hours to get up a palm tree and ten seconds to get back down?"

The farmer takes the tenner and puts it into his pocket. He then takes out a pound coin and hands it to the scientist.

"I don't know," he smiles.

War is hell

At the start of World War One, a father tells his son he has to go and fight for his country. Nodding, his son asks his father to bring him back a German helmet from the battlefields. "You know," says the boy, "one with a spike on top."

And so, weeks later the man is out on the mud-soaked fields of Flanders when he spies a German helmet lying in the mud. Bending down to pick it up, he finds it stuck fast; as he grasps the spike for a better grip, he realises there is a German soldier still attached to it.

"If you pull me out of ze dirt, you can take me prisoner," says the soldier, through the mud.

"If I pull you out," says the Brit, "can I have your helmet for my son?"

"Ja – be my guest!" the German replies.

But, after half an hour, he's still only managed to get the Kraut out up to the waist. "I'm bloody knackered," he says, catching his breath.

"Vud it help," replies the German soldier, "if I took my feet out of ze stirrups?"

After surgery, a man wakes up drowsily in the hospital. He yells to the nurse, "I can't feel my legs!"

"Well, of course you can't," she replies. "You have just had your arms amputated."

Double vision

A drunken old bloke stumbles into the front door of a pub, walks up to the barman and says, "Give me a damn shot of vodka."

The barman tells him that he's had enough, so the old guy swears and walks out the front door.

A few minutes later, the same drunk comes in through the side door and stumbles up to the bar and demands a shot of vodka. The barman looks at him in disbelief and refuses to serve him again. The old man swears again and storms out.

Within minutes the same old bloke stumbles in through the back door and before he can say a word, the barman says, "Listen, I told you already twice that I'm not going to serve you, so get out of my bar, you drunken bastard."

The old guy looks at the bartender and says, "Damn; how many bars do you work at?"

Breathe deeply and relax

The phone at the local hospital rings and the duty medic picks it up to hear a man jabbering on the other end.

"My wife's contractions are only two minutes apart!" he says.

"Is this her first child?" the doctor asks.

"No, you idiot" the man shouts "This is her husband!"

It's funny because it's true

What do you call 300 white men chasing a black man?

The PGA tour.

Smart thinking

An efficiency expert concludes his lecture with a note of caution.

"You need to be careful about trying these techniques at home," he says.

"Why?" asks a man in the audience.

"I watched my wife's routine at breakfast for years," the expert explains. "She made lots of trips between the fridge, cooker, table and cabinets, often carrying a single item at a time. One day I told her, 'Honey, why don't you try carrying several things at once?'"

"Did it save time?" the guy in the audience asked.

"Actually, yes," replies the expert. "It used to take her 30 minutes to make breakfast. Now I do it in ten."

Your number's up

Five Germans in an Audi Quattro arrive at the Italian border. The Italian Customs agent stops them: "It'sa illegala to putta five people in a Quattro."

"Wat do you mean it'z illegal?" asks the German driver.

"Quattro meansa four," replies the Italian official.

"Quattro is just ze name of ze automobile," the German says in disbelief. "Look at ze papers. This car is designed to kerry five."

"You can'ta pulla thata one on me!" replies the Italian. "Quattro meansa four. You hava five people ina your car and you are breakinga tha law!"

The German driver is angry. "You idiot! Call ze supervisor over, I want to speak to somevone with more intelligence!"

"Sorry," says the Italian. "He'sa busy with two guys in a Fiat Uno."

The good news: Saddam Hussein is facing the death penalty.
The bad news: Beckham is taking it...

Speculate to accumulate

After his business goes bust, a redneck called Scooter finds himself in dire financial trouble, and resorts to prayer. "God, please help me," he wails. "I've lost my business, and if I don't get some money, I'm going to lose my car as well. Please let me win the lottery."

Saturday night comes, and Scooter watches aghast as someone else wins. Again, he begins to pray:

"God, please let me win the lottery! I've lost my business, my car, and I'm going to lose my house."

Next Saturday night comes, and Scooter still has no luck. Once again, he prays. "God, why haven't you helped me?" he cries. "I've lost my business, my house, my car, and my children are starving! I've always been a good servant to you; please let me win the lottery just this once!"

Suddenly, there is a blinding flash of light as the heavens open, and Scooter is confronted with the glowing, ethereal vision of God himself.

"Scooter," he booms. "Meet me half-way on this. Buy a ticket."

Grim reality

Heard about the new official Chelsea dartboard?

It comes with no doubles or trebles.

Well, how about that?

An Aussie lass visiting Britain in February stops at a red light behind a trucker. She leaps out of her car, knocks on his window and says: "Hi, my name's Cheryl and you're losing your load."

The trucker shakes his head and drives on. At the next set of traffic lights, she stops behind him, gets out and taps on his window again saying, "Hi; I dunno if you heard me. My name's Cheryl and you're losing your load."

He drives on. At the third set of lights she's still tapping on his window, saying: "Hi, mate; my name's Cheryl and you're losing your load."

Once again he shakes his head and drives on.

At the fourth set of lights, the truck driver leaps out of his cab quickly, goes over to the blonde's car, taps on her window and says, "Hi, Cheryl. My name's Dave, and I'm driving a gritter."

Thanks; I needed to hear that

Brazilian forward Ronaldo walks into a Burger King in Milan and asks for two Whoppers.

"OK," says the cashier. "You're not fat, and you haven't lost it."

> **A golfer was lining up his tee shot.**
> **"What's taking so long?" demanded his partner.**
> **"My wife is watching me from the club house. This needs to be a perfect shot."**
> **"Forget it," said his partner, "you'll never hit her from here."**

Man to man

A deaf mute strolls into a chemist's shop to buy a packet of condoms. Unfortunately the mute cannot see any of his required brands on the shelves, and the chemist, unable to decipher sign language, fails to understand what the man wants. Frustrated, the deaf mute decides to take drastic action. He unzips his trousers and drops his penis on the counter, before placing a £5 note next to it. Nodding, the chemist unzips his own trousers, slaps his mammoth shlong down on the counter next to the mute's pecker, then picks up both notes and stuffs them in his pocket.

The now-furious deaf mute begins to grunt angrily at the chemist, waving his arms wildly.

"Sorry," says the chemist, shrugging his shoulders, "but if you can't afford to lose, you shouldn't gamble."

Members' enclosure

A group of second-, third- and fourth-year primary school kids are accompanied by two women teachers on a field trip to the local racetrack to learn about horses. Soon after arriving it's time to take the children to the toilet, so it's decided that the girls will go with one teacher and the boys with the other.

The teacher assigned to the boys is waiting outside the men's room, when one of the boys comes out and tells her that none of them can reach the urinal. Having no choice, she goes inside, helps the boys with their pants and begins hoisting the little boys up one by one to help them pee.

As she lifts one, she can't help but notice that he's unusually well endowed.

Trying not to show that she was staring, the teacher says, "You must be in the fourth."

"No, miss," he replies in a thick Irish brogue. "I'm in the seventh, riding Silver Arrow, but thanks for the fumble."

A nine-year-old boy walks into a bar and demands the barmaid give him a Scotch on the rocks.

"Hey, do you want to get me into trouble?" the barmaid asks.

"Maybe later," says the kid, "but for now I'll just have my drink."

Accidents will happen

A redneck trucker is driving down the highway when he hears a loud thump under his rig. He stops to check the damage, and then calls his boss.

"I hit a pig on the road, and he's stuck under my truck," he explains. "What should I do?"

"Shoot him in the head," answers the boss. "Then pull him out and throw him in the truck."

The driver does it, and then calls his boss back. "I did what you told me," he explains.

"So what's the problem?" snaps the boss.

The driver replies, "I don't know what to do with his motorcycle."

Scents and sensibility

Two Aussie girls walk up to the perfume counter in a superstore and pick up a sample bottle.

Shazza sprays it on her wrist and smells it: "That's quite nice, don't you think, Cheryl?"

"Yeah; what's it called?" says Cheryl to the assistant.

"*Viens à moi*," comes the reply.

"*Viens à moi*; what does that mean?" asks Shazza.

"*Viens à moi*, ladies, is French for 'come to me'," says the assistant haughtily.

Shazza takes another sniff and offers her arm to Cheryl saying, "That doesn't smell like come to me. Does that smell like come to you, Cheryl?"

Thanks for nothing!

Irish engineers Paddy and Shamus are standing at the base of a flagpole, looking up.

A blonde woman walks by and asks, "What are you doing?"

"We're supposed to find the height of the flagpole," says Shamus, "but we don't have a ladder."

The blonde takes a wrench from her purse, loosens a few bolts, and lays the pole down. Next she pulls a tape measure from her pocket, takes a measurement and announces, "Five metres." She then walks away.

Paddy shakes his head and laughs. "Ain't that just like a blonde, Shamus? We ask for the height and she gives us the length!"

Way to go!

A man turns to his new girlfriend and says, "Since I first laid eyes upon your beautiful body, my darling, I've wanted to make love to you really, really badly."

The girlfriend responds, "Well, you succeeded."

Gasoline Alley

A little girl asks her mother, "Mum, can I take the dog for a walk around the park?"

Mum replies, "No, because the dog's on heat."

"What does that mean?" asks the child.

"Go and ask your father. I think he's in the garage."

The little girl goes to the garage and asks, "Dad, may I take Susie for a walk around the block? I asked Mum, but she said that Susie was on heat, and to come and talk to you."

The dad thinks for a second. He then takes a rag, soaks it with petrol and scrubs the dog's rear end with it. "OK," he says, "you can go now, but keep Susie on the leash."

The little girl leaves. She returns a few minutes later with no dog on the leash.

"Hey, where's Susie?" the dad says.

"She'll be here in a minute," the little girl says. "She ran out of petrol and another dog's pushing her home."

Did you hear about the dogs' home that got broken into?
The police still have no leads.

The finishing touch

A man's father dies, so he goes to the undertaker and tells him he wants the best of everything for his dear old dad.

The man is so upset about his old man's death he can't bring himself to go to the funeral. The next day, he gets a bill for £8,000. He pays it. The next month, he gets another bill for £70. He figures it's just a little supplementary bill, so he pays that, too.

Next month, another bill for £70 arrives, so he calls up the undertaker and says, "I keep getting these bills for £70. I thought I paid for the funeral already."

The undertaker says, "Well, you said you wanted the best for your father, so I rented him a tux."

Money well spent

One Saturday, an older man and a sexy brunette walk into an expensive fur store.

"Show the lady your finest mink coat!" the man tells the owner.

The owner retrieves the store's best mink. The young woman tries it on and loves it.

"Sir," the owner whispers to the man, "that fur costs £25,000."

"No problem," the man replies, "I'll write you a cheque."

"You can pick up the coat on Monday, after the cheque clears," the owner says.

On Monday, the man returns to the store on his own.

"How dare you show your face in here?" the owner screams. "There wasn't a penny in your account!"

"Yeah; sorry about that," the man says with a smile, "but I wanted to thank you for the best weekend of my life!"

A small boy is lost, so he goes up to a policeman and says, "I can't find my dad."

"What's he like?" the policeman enquires.

"Beer and women," replies the boy.

Shaggy humps

Having just arrived at a Foreign Legion outpost, a raw recruit asks the corporal what the men do for recreation. The corporal smiles and says: "You'll see."

The young man is puzzled. "Well, you've got more than 100 men on this base and I don't see a single woman."

"You'll see," the corporal repeats.

That afternoon, 300 camels are herded into the corral. On a signal, the men go wild and sprint into the enclosure to grab a camel. The recruit sees the corporal hurrying past and grabs his arm.

"I don't understand," he says. "There must be over 300 camels and only 100 of us. Why is everybody rushing? Can't a man take his time?"

"What?" exclaims the corporal, wild-eyed. "And get stuck with an ugly one?"

Cherchez la femme

Two men's shopping trolleys collide in a supermarket.

"Sorry," says the first man. "I was looking for my wife."

The second man replies, "Me, too. Let's work together. What does yours look like?"

The first man describes his wife, "She's a tall brunette with a great figure. What about yours?"

The second man thinks for a second, "She'll turn up. Let's look for yours instead."

Howdy, serif

Four fonts walk into a bar.

Barman says: "Oi! Get out! We don't want your type in here!"

Stick it out, man

Did you hear about the man who joined the nudist colony?

The first day was his hardest.

> **Two prostitutes after the Christmas holidays.**
>
> **"What did you ask Santa Claus to give you?" asks one.**
>
> **"Hundred quid, as usual," replies the other.**

Old chap

An attractive woman from New York is driving through a remote part of Texas when her car breaks down. A few minutes later, a cowboy on horseback wearing leather chaps comes along.

"Howdy, ma'am. I'm Pete; can I give you a ride into town?"

The woman accepts, climbs up behind him on the horse and they ride off.

Every few minutes, the cowboy lets out a whoop so loud that it echoes from the surrounding hills. When they arrive in town, he lets her off at a service station and yells one final "Yahoo!" before riding off.

"What did you do to get Pete so excited?" the service-station attendant asks.

"Nothing," she says, "I just sat behind him on the horse, put my arms around his waist and held on to his saddle horn so I wouldn't fall off."

"Lady," the attendant says, "apart from those chaps, Pete rides bareback."

Mutually assured destruction

What's the difference between mechanical engineers and civil engineers?

Mechanical engineers build weapons; civil engineers build targets.

Pin-sharp

An elderly gentleman had serious hearing problems for a number of years. He went to the doctor, and was fitted with a set of hearing aids that allowed him to hear 100 per cent.

A month later, the gentleman went back for a check-up. The doctor said, "Your hearing's perfect. Your family must be really pleased for you."

The gentleman replied, "Oh, I haven't told my family yet. I just sit around and listen to the conversations. I've changed my will three times so far!"

Textbook landing

Qantas Flight 101 is flying from Heathrow to Sydney, with Shayne the pilot and Wayne the co-pilot. As they approach Sydney airport, they look out of the front window.

"Christ," says Shayne. "Will you look how short that runway is? This is going to be one of the trickiest landings you're ever going to see!"

"You're not kidding, mate," replies Wayne.

"Right, Wayne; when I give the signal, you put the engines in full reverse," says Shayne.

So they approach the runway and as soon as the wheels hit the ground, Wayne slams the engines in reverse, puts the flaps down and stamps on the brakes. Amidst roaring engines, squealing tyres and lots of smoke, the plane screeches to a halt inches from the end of the runway, much to the relief of Shayne and Wayne and everyone on board.

As they sit in the cockpit regaining their composure, Shayne looks out the front window and says to Wayne, "That has got to be the shortest runway I've ever seen in my whole life."

Wayne looks out the side window and replies, "Yeah, mate, but look how wide it is!"

Soft in the head

There are two old drunks in a bar. The first one says, "Ya know, when I was 30 and got a hard-on, I couldn't bend it with either of my hands. By the time I was 40, I could bend it about 10 degrees if I tried really hard. By the time I was 50, I could bend it about 20 degrees, no problem. I'm gonna be 60 next week, and now I can almost bend it in half with just one hand"

"So," says the second drunk, "what's your point?"

"Well," says the first, "I'm just wondering how much stronger I'm gonna get!"

A man goes to the doctor and says, "Doctor, I'm having some trouble with my hearing."

"What are the symptoms?" asks the doctor.

The man replies, "A yellow TV cartoon family."

All heart

A big, burly man visited the local vicar's home and asked to see the vicar's wife, a woman well known for her charity work.

"Madam," he said in a broken voice, "I wish to draw your attention to the terrible plight of a poor family in this village. The father is dead, the mother is too ill to work and the nine children are starving. They are about to be turned on to the cold, empty streets unless someone pays their rent, which amounts to £400."

"How terrible!" exclaimed the vicar's wife. "May I ask who you are?"

"I'm their landlord," he sobbed.

Choke chain

What's the difference between James Blunt and a puppy?
  Eventually, the puppy stops whining.

Divorcee of Christ

What's black and white and tells the Pope to get lost?
  A nun who's just won the lottery.

Boys will be boys

What do you call a woman who knows where her husband is?
  A widow.

> **Two buckets of sick are walking down the street. One bursts into tears. "What's the matter?" asks the other.**
>
> **He replies: "This is where I was brought up."**

His hand in marriage

A man comes home from a poker game late one night and finds his wife waiting for him with a rolling pin.

  "Where have you been?" she asks.

"Pack all your bags," he demands. "I lost you in a card game."

"How did you manage to do that?"

"It wasn't easy," he says. "I had to fold a royal flush."

Good enough for me

A local business is looking for office help. They put a sign in the window, stating: "HELP WANTED. Must be able to type, must be good with a computer and must be bilingual."

A short time afterwards, a dog trots up to the window and goes inside. He looks at the receptionist and wags his tail, then walks over to the sign, looks at it and whines. Getting the idea, the receptionist gets the office manager.

The manager says, "I can't hire you. The sign says you have to be able to type."

With that, the dog jumps down, goes to the typewriter and proceeds to type out a perfect letter.

The manager is stunned, but tells the dog, "The sign also says you have to be good with a computer."

The dog jumps down again and goes to the computer, where it enters and executes a spreadsheet perfectly.

By this time the manager is totally dumbfounded. He looks at the dog and says, "I realise that you are a very intelligent dog and have some interesting abilities. However, I still can't give you the job. You have to be bilingual."

The dog looks at the manager calmly and says, "Meow!"

Two cows are standing next to each other in a field. Daisy says to Dolly, "I was artificially inseminated this morning."

"I don't believe you," says Dolly.

"It's true, no bull!"

Back in a mo

Cruising at 40,000 feet, an airplane suddenly shudders and a passenger looks out of the window. "Sh*t!" he screams, "one of the engines just blew up!"

Other passengers leave their seats and come running over. Suddenly the aircraft is rocked by a second blast as yet another engine explodes on the other side.

The passengers are in a panic now, and even the stewardesses can't maintain order. Just then, standing tall and smiling confidently, the pilot strides from the cockpit and assures everyone that there is nothing to worry about. His words and his demeanour make most of the passengers feel better, and they sit down as the pilot calmly walks to the door of the aircraft. There, he grabs several packages from under the seats and hands them to the flight attendants.

Each crew member attaches the package to their backs.

"Say," says an alert passenger, "aren't those parachutes?"

The pilot nods with a smile. The passenger goes on, "But I thought you said there was nothing to worry about?"

"There isn't," replies the pilot as a third engine explodes. "We're just going to get help."

We can only do so much

Tony Blair is visiting an Edinburgh hospital. He enters a ward full of patients with no obvious sign of injury or illness and greets one.

The patient replies:

"Fair fa your honest sonsie face,

Great chieftain o' the puddin race,

Aboon them a' you take your place,

Painch, tripe or thairm,

As lang's my airm."

Blair is confused, so he just grins and moves on to the next patient and says hello.

The patient responds:

"Some hae meat and canna eat,

And some wad eat that want it,

But we hae meat and we can eat,

So let the Lord be thankit."

Even more confused, the PM moves on to the next patient, who immediately begins to chant:

"We sleekit, cowerin, timrous beasty,

Thou needna start awa sae hastie,

Wi' bickering brattle."

Now seriously troubled, Blair turns to the accompanying doctor and asks, "What kind of facility is this? A mental ward?"

"No," replies the doctor. "This is the serious Burns unit."

Reality bites

The Three Bears returned one sunny Sunday morning from a stroll in the woods to find the door of their little house open. Cautiously, they went inside.

After a while, big Daddy Bear's deep voice boomed out, "Someone's been eating my porridge!"

Mummy Bear gave a yelp. "Someone's been eating MY porridge!" she said.

Little Baby Bear rushed in, "Forget the damn porridge; some b*stard's nicked the DVD player!"

That's telling him!

An Asian man walks into the currency exchange in New York City with 2000 yen and walks out with $72. The following week, he walks in with 2000 yen, and is handed $66. He asks the teller why he got less money that week than the previous week.

The teller says, "Fluctuations, sir."

The Asian man storms out, and just before slamming the door, turns around and shouts, "Fluc you Americans, too!"

Virtue rewarded

A man is standing at the Pearly Gates before St. Peter.

"All you need to have done is one good deed, and we will allow you passage into heaven."

The man says, "No problem. I was stopped at a crossroads once and saw a gang of blokes harassing a young woman. I got out of my car, walked up to the leader, who was over seven feet tall and must have weighed nearly 15 stone, and I told him that abusing a woman is a cowardly act and that I would not tolerate it. I then reached up, yanked out his nose ring and kicked him in the balls to make a point."

St. Peter is amazed and starts searching the man's life in his book in front of him and says, "I can't find that incident anywhere in your file. When did that happen?"

The man looks down at his watch and says, "Oh, about two minutes ago."

Quick thinking

A university student delivers a pizza to an old man's house.

"I suppose you want a tip?" says the old man.

"That would be great," says the student, "but the other guy who does deliveries told me not to expect too much; he said if I got 50p, I'd be lucky."

The old man looks hurt. "Well, to prove him wrong, here's £5. What are you studying?"

"Applied psychology," replies the student.

> **You might think life is rubbish, but imagine being an egg.**
> **You only get smashed once, you only get laid once and the only bird to sit on your face is your mother!**

This is going to cost you...

What do you call an Amish guy with his hand up a horse's arse?

A mechanic.

Drawing the line

An armless man walks into a bar, which is empty except for the bartender. He orders a pint of Guinness and, when he is served, asks the bartender if he would get the money from his wallet in his pocket, since he has no arms.

The bartender obliges him. He then asks if the bartender would tip the glass to his lips. The bartender does this until the man finishes his pint. He then asks if the bartender could get a hanky from his pocket and wipe the foam from his lips. The bartender does this, and comments that it must be very difficult not to have any arms and have to ask someone to do nearly everything for him.

The man says, "Yes, it is a bit embarrassing at times. By the way, where's your restroom?"

The bartender quickly replies, "The closest one is in the petrol station down the street."

Differential diagnosis

An attractive young girl, chaperoned by an ugly old lady, enters a doctor's office.

"We've come for an examination," says the young girl.

"All right," says the doctor. "Go behind that curtain and take your clothes off."

"No, not me," says the girl, "it's my old aunt here."

"Very well," says the doctor. "Madam, stick out your tongue."

It's elementary

Why should you never replace your sandwich toaster?

Better the Breville you know.

No sprain, no gain

A man goes to his local gym to ask about yoga classes for beginners.

The instructor asks, "How flexible are you?"

"Well," replies the man, "I can't do Wednesdays."

> **What is the worst thing that can happen to a bat while asleep?**
> **The runs.**

Rash decision

Did you hear about the New Zealand farmer who thought he had an STD?

It turns out that he was just allergic to wool.

Rabbiting in the headlights

An Essex girl was driving down the A13 when her car phone rang.

It was her boyfriend, urgently warning her, "Treacle, I just heard on the news that there's a car going the wrong way on the A13. Please be careful!"

"It's not just one car!" said the Essex girl. "There's hundreds of them!"

What has four legs and an arm?
A happy rottweiler.

I asked you first

A copper pulls a guy over for speeding and notices his eyes are red.

He says, "Hello, sir. I see your eyes look red. Have you been drinking?"

The driver replies, "Hello, officer. I see your eyes look glazed. Have you been eating doughnuts?"

Keep death off the roads

How do you blind a woman?
Put a windscreen in front of her.

Sonar, and yet so far

What did the fisherman say to the magician?
  "Pick a cod: any cod."

Tactical withdrawal

How many Frenchmen does it take to defend Paris?
  It's never been tried.

Man of business

What does a pimp put on his CV as a job title?
  Holesaler.

Thanks anyway

A golfer is looking for a new caddy one day when his friend says, "I know a great caddy; he's 90 years old but he has eyes like a hawk."

"OK, then," says the man, "tell him I'm playing again in a week."

The week passes and they start to play. The golfer hits a perfect drive. He is so pleased with himself that he holds his follow-through position for several moments. Unwinding, he says to the caddy, "Did you see where it went?"

The caddy says, "I sure did."

"Great; where is it?"

The caddy replies, "I don't remember."

Hot pursuit

Two Aussie girls, Sheila and Kylie, are out driving in a new sports car.

"Look out for cops," says Sheila. "I'm going to see how fast we can go."

After five miles of driving like Jenson Button, Sheila looks across at Kylie and asks, "Can you see any cops?"

"Yes," Kylie replies.

"Are their lights on?" says Sheila.

Kylie thinks for a moment, and then says: "Yes. No. Yes. No. Yes. No."

Double the fun

Why is the space between a woman's breasts and her hips called a waist?

Because you could easily fit another pair of breasts in there.

Quick learner

A customer at Morris' Gourmet Grocery marvelled at the proprietor's quick wit and intelligence.

"Tell me, Morris; what makes you so smart?"

"I wouldn't share my secret with just anyone," Morris replies, lowering his voice so the other shoppers won't hear, "but, since you're a good and faithful customer, I'll let you in on it. Fish heads: you eat enough of them, you'll be positively brilliant."

"You sell them here?" the customer asks.

"Only £4 apiece," says Morris.

The customer buys three. A week later, he's back in the store complaining that the fish heads were disgusting and he isn't any smarter.

"You didn't eat enough," says Morris.

The customer goes home with 20 more fish heads. Two weeks later, he's back and this time he's really angry.

"Hey, Morris," he says, "You're selling me fish heads for £4 apiece when I just found out I can buy the whole fish for £2. You're ripping me off!"

"You see?" says Morris. "You're smarter already."

An Englishman, an Irishman, a Scotsman, a Catholic, a Jew and a blind man walk into a pub.
The landlord says: "Is this some kind of joke?"

Fatal extraction

A man walks into a dentist's office and says, "I think I'm a moth."

The dentist replies, "You shouldn't be here. You should be seeing a psychiatrist."

The man replies, "I am seeing a psychiatrist."

The dentist says, "Well, then, what are you doing here?"

The man says, "Your light was on."

Tall story

What do giraffes have that no other animal can possibly have?
  Baby giraffes!

A dyslexic goth sold his soul to Santa.

A dyslexic rock star choked on his own Vimto.

A dyslexic went to a toga party... as a goat.

Fanny peculiar

A coachload of OAPs is out on a day trip travelling around the country. Suddenly, without warning, one of the old ladies leaps into the air. "I've just been molested!" she screams.

The coach driver stops the coach, "But we're down a country lane in the middle of nowhere!" he says. "Did any one else see anything?"

All the other old folk on the coach shake their heads, and as things settle down the driver heads off again.

A couple of miles along the road, the same old lady leaps into the air, "I've been molested again! Stop the coach!"

This time, the driver, wondering if she might be a little bit senile, walks back to her seat and has a look underneath.

To his amazement, there's an old, bald chap curled up in the footwell, squinting up at him.

"What the hell are you doing?" asks the driver.

"I haven't got my glasses and I'm looking for my toupée," the old geezer replies, "I almost had it twice, but it got away both times!"

Better luck next time

Why is the Premiership like a cordless drill?
No Leeds.

Still anyone's game

What do you call two Mexicans playing basketball?
Juan on Juan

Hooks, mon

What do you call a Scottish cloakroom attendant?
Angus McCoatup.

Green tee

What do you call Kate Moss with a swollen toe?
A golf club.

Cupboard love

What do you call ten lesbians in a closet?
A liquor cabinet.

Sign of the times

A guy walks into a pub and orders a drink. After a few more, he needs to go to the toilet. He doesn't want anyone to steal his drink so he puts a sign on it saying, "I spat in this beer, do not drink!" After a few minutes, he returns and there's another sign next to his beer saying, "So did I!"

Somebody complimented me on my driving the other day. They left me a note on my windscreen saying, "Parking Fine." So that was nice.

Hidden talents

Two buddies are sitting in a singles' club and talking about another guy sitting at the other end of the bar. "I don't get it," complained the first guy. "He's not good-looking, he has no taste in clothes, drives a beat-up wreck of a car, yet he always manages to go home with the most beautiful women here!"

"Yeah," replies his buddy. "He's not even very good conversationally – all he does is sit there and lick his eyebrows."

Better fold your tray table

A pompous priest is seated next to a redneck on a flight across the US. After the plane is airborne, drink orders are taken.

"I'll have a Jack Daniels and Coke," says the redneck.

When it's the priest's turn to place his order he looks at the redneck in disgust and says, "I'd rather be savagely raped by brazen whores than let alcohol touch these lips."

The redneck hands his drink back to the flight attendant and says, "Me, too. I didn't realise we had a choice!"

Apart from that...

A man's eating lunch in a restaurant when he has cause to call the waiter over: "I've got some bad news and some worse news," he says. "Which do you want to hear first?"

The waiter opts to hear the bad news first.

"The bad news is there's a fly in my soup," says the diner.

"OK; what's the worse news?" enquires the waiter.

"It's the best part of the meal."

I knew that!

President Bush is rehearsing his speech for the Beijing 2008 Olympic Games. He begins with "Ooo! Ooo! Ooo! Ooo! Ooo!"

Immediately, his speechwriter rushes over to the lectern and whispers in the president's ear: "Mr President, those are the Olympic rings. Your speech is underneath."

Prix d'Or

Did you hear about the man who collected five thousand door knockers?

He won a no-bell prize.

Bogged down

During training exercises, a British Army lieutenant is driving down a muddy back road and encounters another jeep stuck in the mud with a red-faced colonel at the wheel.

"Your jeep stuck, sir?" asks the lieutenant as he pulled alongside.

"Nope," replies the colonel, coming over and handing him the keys,

"Yours is."

How can you tell if you are at a redneck wedding?

Everyone sits on the same side of the church.

Beach bombs

Two seagulls were flying over the beach at a seaside resort one boiling hot August Bank Holiday afternoon. Every way they looked, there were so many people there wasn't a speck of sand to be seen.

"Ah," said one to the other contemptuously, "takes all the skill out of it, doesn't it?"

Tinkling the ivories

What do you call a man with no arms or legs playing the piano?

A clever dick.

Dirty secret

How do you spot a rebel Amish teenager?

He has a secret stash of pictures of women without bonnets.

Lady garden

A man and a woman started to have sex in the middle of a dark forest. After about 15 minutes of it, the man finally gets up and says, "Damn, I wish I had a torch!"

The woman says, "Me too; you've been eating grass for the past ten minutes!"

Sensible chap

Why was the exhibitionist drinking window-cleaning fluid?

To stop himself from streaking.

The geeks had a word for it

There was a young man who wanted to become a great writer. When asked to define 'great', he said, "I want to write stuff that people will react to on a truly emotional level – stuff that will make them cry and howl in pain and anger!"

He now works for Microsoft, writing error messages.

Why do housewives love Arsenal so much?
Because they stay on top for so long, but always come second.